Lynnee Breedlove's
ONE FREAK SHOW

QueeR cafe presents...

Lynnee Breedlove's
"ONE FREAK SHOW"

queer, punkrock,
standup comedy
from the
Tribe8 legend

+ screening
Lynnee's new film

GODSPEED

a speed freak bike
messenger who
passes as a boy
fights the world and
his own lust for thrills
to win the love of a
stripper

£5

Weds 25th March, 9 Bath Buildings (off cheltenham rd)
doors open 7.30pm, pay at the door

Lynnee Breedlove's
ONE FREAK SHOW

Lynn Breedlove

Manic D Press
San Francisco

Cover illustration: Apaulo Hart   Front cover photo: Kirsten Buchwald
Poster photos: Kael T. Block   Back cover photo: Barbara Price

Library of Congress Cataloging-in-Publication Data

Breedlove, Lynn.
  Lynnee Breedlove's one freak show / Lynn Breedlove.
    p. cm.
  ISBN 978-1-933149-32-5 (trade pbk. : alk. paper)
1. Homosexuality--Humor. 2. Transgender people--Humor. 3. Gay wit and
humor. 4. Breedlove, Lynn. I. Title. II. Title: One freak show.
  PN6231.H57B74 2009
  818'.607--dc22
                        2009024493

Contents

CONFESSIONS OF A POSER

*Dedicated
to
Joe Lee*

IN THE BEGINNING...

When I was a kid, my dad would drive me around in his Chevy station wagon, listening to comedians like George Carlin, Redd Foxx, Rodney Dangerfield, and Don Rickles on AM radio. I didn't know what the hell was so funny, but I wanted to make people laugh like they did.

I had my first chance to make people laugh at a performance for parents at the end of day camp, when I got to play a boy in The Enlarging Machine. Everyone walked by a sheet painted like a machine, with a small hole in one end and a big one in the other. Kids threw in a stick or a pebble—out came a log or a rock. I walked around sneaky—whistling, shifty—then spit in it, and out came a bucket of water on my head. Everyone cracked up. I'm sold. People laughing *with* me instead of *at* me—that was new.

In high school, I memorized and impersonated Flip Wilson's Geraldine Jones routine, "The Devil Made Me Buy This Dress," breaking the cardinal rule of comedy: never do another comic's material. But I got an A on my drama final, and then was asked to perform it again for the senior talent show. As a clueless kid in 1977, I was somehow able to get away with being a white dyke playing a black man playing a black female from the 'hood.

My favorite part of being lead singer for Tribe 8 was in between songs when I got to squeeze in two or three funny lines. The band would watch videos of our gigs after the shows. They'd fast-forward through me introducing the songs, stopping right at the part when they would be onstage yelling, "Less talk, more rock," but I would say, "Stop! I wanna hear what I said."

I never knew what I was saying. I was clean and sober, but being onstage was my drug, so I would spout all this hilarity in some sort of punk blackout and then try to study myself later like a football coach dissecting a game afterwards, and see if anything was salvageable.

Once at the Chameleon in the mid-'90s, Bucky Sinister was hosting an all-boy spoken word night. He invited a bunch of Sisterspitters. The guys all heckled any brilliant writers who got up with anything serious, like Anna Joy, who was my girlfriend at the time and God's gift. So when I got up and threw a set list at my feet, I was ready. "Heckle me, motherfuckers," I said. "I fucking love it." I had the power of the mic and after years of playing to dumbfucks around the world, I knew how to hurl a snappy comeback. I quieted them down with a flurry of verbal violence aimed right over their heads.

When I was on tour with Sisterspit in 1998, like the other eleven writers on tour, I read my words from the page. There was this one person always stretching on the floor before going on stage while everyone else was reading. In an old skool aviator's cap with goggles, she would channel a crazy character, swimming and flying around the stage, freestyling based on stuff she had written, but different every time. That was Stanya Kahn. She had been part of a theater collective in San Francisco in the '80s. I interrogated her about what she did. I would be writing what I was going to read, sometimes up to the last minute before I got onstage, but I always stopped to watch Stanya, fascinated. I never thought I could do what she did.

At Theatre Rhinoceros in 2000, I hosted Kris Kovick's show, where she read from her writing. As host, I talked about my life in San Francisco, sharing all the funny stories I had told for years in bars for free. Kris and I were in the bathroom getting ready one night, and she said to me, "I could never do what you do, fly without a net." It was just what I had thought about Stanya.

When my band was winding down to a dull roar by 2002, I got a show at Rutgers University at a feminist conference with author Erika Lopez. Sick of being stuck to the page, I walked around the parking lot for an hour, thinking, then jotted down some ideas, got up in front of thirty people and made them laugh. That became the prototype of the One Freak Show.

Around that time, I would go around the corner to visit Ren Volpe, an ex of mine with a two-year-old, get wired up on coffee and run my mouth. She kept saying, "You need to put on a one-man show."

I was working at the Montclair Women's Cultural Arts Club and got to pick up one of my favorite dyke comics, Suzanne Westenhoefer, from the airport. I interrogated her like I did Stanya. She said she was a natural, but there is a science. She said, "Always say the opposite of what it is: if the traffic is gnarly, say it was great." Little hints like that, which I remembered. I still listen to her like I listened to Flip Wilson's records, over and over, laughing out loud.

Going to Tarin Tower's comedy night at Spanganga in the Mission that same year, as usual I was making up jokes right up to the front door. I walked onstage in front of a bunch of local male comics, and laid on them what would become the opening line of my *One Freak Show*. After they had spent the evening laughing at each other's poop jokes, they cracked up, which I took as a badge of honor.

Jim Fourniadis was there, running tech, and he asked me if I was a comic and what was I doing? And I said, "Nothing, really." So he invited me to develop a one-man show at his new theater around the corner, The Dark Room. I spent two weeks in the summer of 2003 doing that, calling it *Lynnee Breedlove's One Freak Show: Less Rock, More Hilarity.* I would just make a set list, lay it on the stage at my feet like I had done in the band, and try out every idea I had, to see what would make people laugh.

The following summer (2004), I did the same thing again, fine-tuning it. I asked playwright Bayla Travis to direct me. She helped me delineate the characters of my mom and The Biz, and to get me to take up a little more of the stage. I was used to standing in one place, grabbing a mic stand to ground me so I didn't fly up off the stage and forget all the words, ADD-style. I had to be really reined in, always trying to remember even the words of songs I had been singing for fifteen years in the band. (Too many drugs in the '80s.) And now I had to remember a bunch of words that didn't even rhyme—with no breaks, no one to bounce off of—for an hour, sometimes two. Actually I found that once I got up there, you couldn't shut me up. I had songs (in case I missed rhyming) with beats by Skye Lark. I had stuffed animals. Russian nesting dolls. Eggbeaters. Knives.

Then I started doing walking Tonglen meditation before each show, breathing in fear and breathing out love—all woo-woo—for myself; for every letter in the LGBTIQQAA community; then for the Iraqi children; then for Rove, Cheney, and Bush. And I found that telling jokes in I-statements, with love in my heart for everyone who might or might not be in the audience, made people laugh more.

After doing my show for three years, I googled "How to Write a Joke" and figured out how to do set-up lines and punch lines and callbacks, which I had already been doing instinctively. I learned comedy like I learned German, doing it by ear as long as I could stand it, and then taking a couple of grammar classes.

I went through the whole script, tweaking, rearranging the parts where I knew people should be laughing but they hadn't been, and then did my show at a little San Francisco theater on Valencia Street... punch line, punch line, punch line! It was tight. I was sure they would give me a run. At the end of the night, I hit up the manager. She said, "That's stand-up. We don't do stand-up."

Of course, it wasn't stand-up. Too many props for stand-up. But too many laughs for theater.

Whatever it was, I decided to tour Europe. My extra-femme burlesque girlfriend, Wendy Delorme, did the French translation, which started out as subtitles because she was too shy to get on stage. But after a failed attempt at keeping up with my improv by shining a PowerPoint version of the script on the wall with words that didn't have anything to do with what was physically happening onstage (confusing everyone more), she brought the script onstage and sat off to the side with a mic. Eventually Wendy knew the show well enough to improv with me, and our banter on genderfuck kept French audiences in stitches. Except for those old-school feminists who afterwards informed us we were too binary.

Europe, especially France, is about fifteen years behind San Francisco in the Queer Feminist Theory department. So we set about updating them, one city at a time. One thing my American ass didn't have, that the French did, was a *pisse debout*. One night after my show at a punk venue in Paris, a butch punk—inspired by my men's room routine—handed me her own Freelax. That was the start of delivering punch lines while pissing in a bucket every night.

Each nation's trans-later had their own style. In France, it was extra cute, because the translator was my girlfriend and we had a lot of time to work on the script and make up words in French, like *testichones* for *breasticles*. The French speak no English. So I would talk, they would stare. Then Wendy would say the line, and they would crack up. We got good at that rhythm.

In Italy, the translator, Roberta Cortese, was a straight actress with perfect English. No English speakers in that audience either. I talked. Blank stares. She talked. Uproarious laughter.

In Germany, Sandra Ortman (my friend, the German dyke), insisted on doing it right. I was like, "How 'bout funny?"

She didn't care about funny. She needed it to be perfect. I said, "Make up words." She said, "No way." I said, "This is funny. Translate this part."

"It will not be funny," she said. Okay. In Germany, everyone understands English. So I talked. They laughed. She talked. Blank stares.

In Poland, I got to the punk festival, and they were like, "Translator? We didn't know you needed a translator. Okay, here's two." They carefully listened to me explain the script for four hours, then stationed themselves stage right for the show. I started talking. Silence. I looked over at them. They were completely engrossed in the show. I said, "Well? Translate!" One looked at the other and said, "I thought you were listening." "Oh. I thought you were." Never mind.

That was *One Freak Show*. After translating that script into so many languages, emailing it ahead, then sitting with the person in each country, going through all the layers of differences in the language, culture, and then queer culture, and then comedy itself, I decided the second one-freak show, *Confessions of a Poser*, would just tour where people spoke English. And it would be multimedia.

I had dumped the rapping by now, edging toward real comedy, but also theater. Slides. Music. I would bring a flipchart and draw pictures in Austria, Sweden, Germany. A picture of a meat bee. That's the punch line.

But in the UK, I thought, they speak English, won't need drawings there. Wrong. Apparently they needed pictures in the UK, and in Philly, to understand me. Apparently wherever I go, just talking to shopkeepers, I need to bring a flipchart and a Sharpie.

My pride and joy was when one woman at the Stonewall pointed out, "Very Lenny Bruce." Another record I could listen to forever—*To Is A Preposition, Come Is A Verb*— "D'ja come? D'ja come good?"

When I was blond, I was compared to Ellen DeGeneres, 'cause ya seen one blond visibly queer comic, ya seen 'em all. But my heroes are Dave Chapelle, Flip Wilson, and Richard Pryor, because I like to think I am blazing the same kind of revolutionary trail, poking so they laugh till it hurts *because* it hurts, talking to my people and those who oppress them, so we can all walk out the door together, feeling a little less like killing each other or ourselves.

SEPT 1962

COMMUNITY, WHAT DOES THAT WORD MEAN?

All my homos in the house, all my trannies, all my sensitive guys! Wave your feet in the air like you just don't care.

A small stuffed pig in a tiny leather jacket: "Me, me! I, I!"

A stuffed we-don't-know-what: "Center of the universe, piece o' shit."

"I can dish it out, I can't take it."

"I'm sensitive."

"You shut up."

"No, you shut up."

"No, you shut up."

"No, you shut up... "

I like to impersonate my community by puppeteering small tiny stuffed animals while singing scary songs. Calms people down.

They wear little outfits. As RuPaul says, "We're born naked, the rest is drag." Not to be confused with gender, drag is fun.

Meet the stuffies. Squishy on the inside, tough on the outside. The unidentifiable beastie with a patch over his eye identifies as a pirate. Name is Hello Pirate. Pronouns are "argh" and "aye."

The pig identifies as a biker fag. Hangs out at The Eagle, world famous BDSM bar with branches in every major American city. If you're queer and lost in Chicago, just get directions to The Eagle and click your heels three times. There's no place like home.

Biker Fag Piglet and Hello Pirate like to play military games.

"Get down and gimme twenty."

"Sir, I'm proud to be a maggot, Sir. One, and two, and three, and four..."

Here's a bunny. Identifies as a pitbull. But nobody knows. Except his boyfriend, a bear that identifies as a bumblebee.

Sheep... you'd never know before surgery and hormones ...was a shark.

Small dog that identifies as a baby snow seal. Pop off the snowseal hoodie and... look! You never know what you're dealing with. Could be one sitting next to you right now.

Whenever Biker Fag Piglet is hanging out with the small dog that identifies as a baby snow seal, he gets a sudden urge to bludgeon him to death. Don't worry, it's consensual. He was asking for it in that outfit.

Pirate: "I don't know if tattooing *I consent* on my forehead counts..."

Pig (looks at Lynnee): "What do you think, pal?"

Lynnee: "That's Mr. Pal to you."

Pirate: "Ahem. As I was saying…"

Pig: "Put a sock in it, I'm talking."

Pirate: "Oh, were you talking? I wasn't listening."

Pig: "I'm sensitive!"

WRONG BATHROOM

People are always asking if I'm a man or a woman.

What are they asking *me* for? Do I look like I know? I'm obviously confused. I'm baffled by the most basic daily activities, like going to the public restroom. Society's trying to help by marking the doors with symbols that are totally meaningless. Stick figure. Stick figure with a triangle. Okay, I got a triangle, but it doesn't go that way. Fine, close enough.

But, ladies, why so angry? I understand you're protective of your space, but you won the revolution in the '70s: Billy Jean King beat Bobby Riggs.

Every time I go in the ladies' room, there's some little old lady swinging her handbag at me, yelling, "SECURITY! There's a man in the ladies' room."

I flash her a titty.

"SECURITY! There's a man with tits in the ladies' room."

Fight or flight. In an emergency, your brain dredges up shit your parents told you, shit you never thought you'd use, like "You see your fag friends? How zey valk, *und* sit, *und* stand? Zat's ladylike. Do zat." My mom's from Berlin. She identifies as Marlene Dietrich. Leave my mom out of this and I'll leave this out of your mom. Okay, I'm ready.

Back to the ladies' room. Swish in there, hand on hip, other one waving in the air. "Girlene! Do I ever have to use the little girl's room! Tinkle, tinkle! No, she didn't. Yes, she did." Snap, snap, snap.

"SECURITY! There's a fag in the ladies' room."

It's totally safe in the men's room. They've got Men's Room Rules. Like Elevator Rules. In the elevator, you can look one of three places: you can look at the wall, you can look at the numbers, you can look at your shoes. But you can't turn to the guy next to you and conversate. "Oh, getting off at Ladies Lingerie, huh? Is that for the little lady or is that for you?"

In the men's room, it's the same as in the elevator. Say nothing. Look straight ahead. At the urinal, you can look one of three places. You can look at the wall in front of you, you can look at your stuff, you can move your eyes to the right to see if that guy's stuff is bigger. Wah. You can move your eyes to the left to see if that guy's stuff is smaller. Yeah. But you can't look anybody in the face because that means you're gay.

So I walk right in like I own the place, knowing no one's gonna look at me. Someone's looking at me. It's the gay guy. I know he's not gonna say, "Omigod, you guys! There's a chick in the men's room."

He knows they'll say, "What are you lookin' at them for? What are you? Gay?" And then everyone gets beat up.

So I wink at him as I slip into the stall, singing, "We are family... I got all my LGBTLMNOPQRST community and me."

If you go into the stall, stand up, and make pissing-standing-up sounds. Like a waterfall. Because if you sit down to piss, that means you're gay. Unless you live in northern Europe, where there has been a decades-long campaign to teach boy children to piss sitting down. Then sitting down to piss just means your girlfriend's a feminist, and that means you're whipped.

In American gay bars, there are international *No Blow Jobs* signs in the men's room. In Germany, women's bathrooms have international *No Pissing Standing Up* signs. German feminists are cold. A guy's got one thing going for him, and you take it away.

When you come out of the stall, act casual. Be confident. Don't make excuses. Don't say, "I would have used the urinal, but I got a Prince Albert and I didn't wanna spray ya."

LE PISSE DEBOUT (la peese daboo)

If you want to walk right up and use the urinal, use what the French call the *pisse debout*. Means "piss standing up." They're real poets like that.

The *pisse debout* is called a Freelax in America. It's unwieldy to carry around, and wears a weird hole in your pocket like you got a pointy dick. It needs a holster. There's no way to carry it discreetly.

Since it's so indiscreet anyway, I like to take it all the way and personalize it with some punkrock tape that has little red and black hearts and spades and clubs and diamonds all over it, to remind me that going in the men's room is always a gamble.

What I love about the Freelax *pisse debout* is the large opening. There are a few designs out there, evolving at a high rate of speed as transmen around the world (mainly in Canada) desperately work night and day to make a dick that both pisses and packs. We've come a long way from cutting up and screwing off the lid of a toothpaste tube to earn our place at the stinky trough of mankind.

You can get a fairly realistic Cyberskin squishy dick with a tube through it. Comes in pink or brown. Bendy. But so far in the technological drive for pissing/passing perfection, the tiny opening of this design is a problem. You've got your packy in your pants and all of two seconds to fumble the tiny opening up over your stuff, no looking. Do it right... or you're pissing down your leg. Unless you were a '70s feminist reclaiming your body from the patriarchy and exploring your genitalia by squatting over a mirror naked, you don't know where the hell your piss comes out.

Vaginas are complicated. Things go in here, babies come out here, pee comes out there, as well as some other stuff when you touch here and here just right, that we are not sure whence it originates. Some parts of the vag, like no other body parts in creation, have no other function but fun. You need a map with arrows for all the parts of a pussay. That's right, I said, "pussay." If you want to get laid, you have to say it like that. Don't say "pussy." Definitely do not say, "I want to eat your pussy." You'll never get any. Say, "Yo, can I get some pussaaayyy..."

With the *pisse debout*, the part that goes over your junk is so big, you can unbutton your fly and easily slam it up over your entire area. You don't have to look, you know where your junk is, you don't have to feel around. Wham, slap the back edge of the *pisse debout* an inch in front of your asshole, press up, and form a seal. Everyone knows where their asshole is. Why can't cunts be as simple as assholes? It's right there, boom-ba. It's got a little star: ASSHOLE HERE.

When you start, keep your feet together. Once you've got your stuff all sealed on all sides but the front (so that pee will be forced out the little trough poking out of your jeans), spread your stance like a fag in watersports porn.

Now relax. Even though no one's looking, you're not used to draining the lizard in public. So just breathe, and press down on the front of the *pisse debout* with your thumb, so it looks like a willy. With a thumbnail.

If they do look at your shit, don't start trouble, like, "What are ya, gay?" or, "Yo, eyes on your own work, you're pissin' on my shoes."

More like, "What, never saw a guy with a dickechtomy?"

Or whistle the national anthem. Then say, "I got it blown off in Iraq. All I got left is this li'l plastic spout and you're gonna stare?" Stops questions dead. Don't ask, don't tell.

Pissing standing up will give you compassion for guys who miss. It's hard to aim. Just try. Takes practice, focus. After a few beers, you're concentrating really hard, someone opens the door, you turn to see who it is, and dang, all over the floor.

Looks like a dude can aim perfectly at cute furry things running through the wilderness, but put a toilet bowl in front of us, and suddenly we don't feel like it anymore. Although, those of us born without the equipment seem more adept at its operation, as we do not take it for granted, waving it all around drunk. After parties, you are busy cleaning puddles around the bowl.

This is solved with a simple cork. Before the party, drop it in the toilet. When peeing standing up, no man can resist a target, no matter how drunk. It floats so it never goes down, so the next guy will try to hit the cork, too, even if by chance one of us happens to flush.

I used to think it was Dudes With Dicks (DWD) that were born with a biological impulse to aim. Then I thought, no, it is inspired by the very act of pissing standing up. Once I discovered the *pisse debout*, I tried to hit everything. I even tried to clean other people's skid marks off the toilet bowl with my stream. But that's just some OCD metrosexual thing. Taking a poll, I discovered that aiming is, in fact, a dude thing, because when my femme girlfriend uses my Freelax out in the street, the only thing she aims to do is miss her shoes.

My tool of choice is only $3, and the squishy packer style is $85. Also, you pull the *pisse debout* out of your pocket when you need it, whereas, when I started out, the Piss'n'Pack didn't have a harness, you just plopped it in your tighty-whities. But I don't wear tighty whities, I wear boxers. That shit can fall out. And when your dick drops out of your pantleg on the street, you got to keep walking. "That shit ain't mine."

WOORRRRK!

It's a tough world. You gotta stay in shape. Stay healthy. I don't go to the gym. The world is my gym. Everyday circumstances are my workout routine. To stay physically (as well as mentally) fit, I also boost my immune system, which is crucial for survival in today's world. I work out by pissing in the urinal for the mental challenge, after sitting down in the men's room stall to build the immune system.

Then for an advanced workout, I hit the public payphones. Walk up to a phone, nonchalant, like you're gonna call somebody. Lick it. Hang up. Walk away.

The next week—don't do this all in one day, you gotta work up to it slow—you go to the Greyhound bus station or General Assistance office, and find a whole row of phones. Lick one. Hang up. Lick the next one. Hang up. Grab one in each hand:

lick, lick, hang up. Crack your neck. Look scary. Shadowbox.

The next week do ten reps of each and head over to the down escalator. Squat down. Lean forward. Stick out your tongue. Hit that hand railing. Eye of the tiger. Don't nobody fuck with me. Anybody fuck with you, you tell 'em Lynnee "Don't Nobody" Breedlove is your baby daddy.

You can't be shopping at Whole Paycheck, eating organic: you'll get soft. Hurricanes, earthquakes, terrorism—you got to stay in shape, be ready for anything, you never know what danger lurks around the next corner. For example, they just made it illegal to be transgender at the airport. It's masquerading as the other gender, going in disguise. If your outfit doesn't match your body, you're going to jail for being a sneaky terrorist:

"Here's your maggot soup, terrorist."

"Um, hi, I ordered the organic kale and tofu?"

When the nukes hit the fan, who's gonna be left? Mr. Pal and the cockroaches, pal, not you. Why? Because of the Phone Licking.

I also challenge my coordination skills, first thing in the morning. You're probably already working out right now. You make coffee before you've had any? Next week, do like me and buy coffee filters the wrong size. Then whip out the scissors and cut them to fit the coffee machine... before coffee.

I've been training ever since I was a little kid. My first personal trainer, Dad, would wake me up for school by snapping open the blinds, searing my retinas with morning sun, singing songs from *Oklahoma.* "Oh, what a beautiful morning..."

Straight guys who like musicals are called metrosexuals. I

don't think my dad identifies as a metrosexual though. Watch out about labeling others unconsensually, you might get smacked with a handbag or a golf club.

Ever since those early childhood morning workouts, to stay in shape, I keep posing extra added challenges for myself. First, I advertise on Craigslist for roommates. Then, I put in the ad that I love morning people, the ones with the spring-loaded eyeballs who wake up and immediately start enunciating and projecting before they get out of bed. "GOOD MORNING! I HAVEN'T TALKED TO ANYONE FOR EIGHT HOURS AND BOY, I CAN'T WAIT TO GET STARTED!"

One eye open, I'm cutting up coffee filters, "Mornin'."

The next week, I work up to calling people. Before coffee. From bed. People that might not be that supportive.

"Hi, collections? Yeah, it's Mr. Pal. You know that money I owe you? Still don't have it. When will I? September... 2050."

Looking, looking, for a worthy sparring partner. The IRS... Nah, too easy...

"Hi, Mom? Hey, I got a show tonight. I know, too many F-words. My field's flooded? Right, everyone's a comedian. Okay, I'll go to the post office. And fill out an application."

EXTRA REAL REALITY TV

Gotta be in shape. Stay sharp. Be ready. We're tough in our neighborhood. Reality TV. Whose reality is that? Follow me around with a camera. I got your harsh reality. In *Survivor*: close up on some maggots, then cut to terrified face of a guy trying to figure out how to eat them. In *Punk Survivor*: close up on utility bills, cut to my terrified face, trying to figure out how to pay them.

Then there's *Cribs*. Follow a notorious heavy metal drummer who lives in Malibu up a two-mile driveway as he points to his Sportster. Follow him into the orgy room. "I banged all three *Charlie's Angels* here last week. 'Cept for Drew. Her and my old lady disappeared for a while."

To fur-lined bathroom. That's not practical. What if he wanks off all over the wall? Oh yeah, he has people. When you're that rich, you never have to jerk off again.

Giant bed in movie room. Starfucks stand manned by a barrista. Kitchen. Fridge, $200-an-ounce food never seen before, from Whole Paycheck. "No Mr. Carb in here!" He lifts his shirt and flashes ab-age.

My reality home show isn't *Cribs*. The kitchen is not designer. It's not even Bloodbath and Beyond our Means. "On this episode of MTV *Squats...*"

We hear Black Flag blasting. "I'm Lynnee Breedlove, this is my pit bull. Pet at your own risk."

Follow Lynnee down Crack Alley. Close up on crowbar opening boarded-up door. "Now we're gonna check out my entry hall."

Shot of boombox on floor. "Here's what we call 'CBGB West.'"

Still in same room. "Now to the love nest, ladies." Pan to seedy mattress. "This is where the magic happens. Not to brag," winks at the camera. "Exact location of a five-dollar BJ from a Capp Street lady of the night." Zoom in on empty condom package.

"Now I'm gonna show you where I hang out the most." Shot of bucket in corner. "The bathroom. Ooh, gotta empty that... And what's the point of having a kitchen if you're not gonna have a bitchin' fridge?" Zoom in on Styrofoam cooler, as lid is lifted to reveal...

"Iceberg lettuce has a shelf life of six months. No Mr. Carb in here. Except for the PBR—Pabst Smear Ribbon, bitches!"

The Swan was a TV show where perfectly fine but depressed babes reported to the camera that their old man wouldn't do them, their kids hated them, and their parents ignored them. The solution? Go stand naked in front of a male plastic surgeon. "One breast's lower than the other, we'll have to fix that..."

Oh yeah, Doc? Let's see what you got. One huevo's hanging lower than the other. Extreme makeover, right now. Nurse? Box cutter.

The makeover show I would like to see would be *The Eagle*. Girlfriend sits arms folded, mad. Next to her, Poor Little Butchie Butch slumps in front of the football game, unemployed. Drunk. Stupified. Unfashionable. Her dog pisses on her leg.

Cut to Butch being wheeled out of surgery bandaged from neck to groin. "Just shoot me. Morphine. Help." He disappears down the hall on wheels.

Over the next three months: gym, therapist, hairdresser, T shots, nicotine gum, AA, a résumé, a trip to Toys in Babeland and the Harley store.

And now the unveiling: curtains open, and ta-dah! Gay pornstar in a suit. His girlfriend, pals, and dog all cry and hump his leg. He walks right past his old lady, and heads offstage with his best brofriend.

If you keep stepping up the challenges everyday, you can get awesome. If you really want a challenge, date a New Yorker: a personal trainer for your ego. I was all over this badass New Yorker chick once. She said, "Get awesome!" I jumped up and flexed, posing, showing off muscles.

"What are you doing?"

"You told me to get awesome. I'm getting awesome."

"I *said*, 'Get *off* me.' "

ALPHABET CITY

My biggest challenge is pronouncing the unpronounceable acronym of the queer community, LGBTIQQ. Why all these letters? Let me explain:

It used to be simple. We started out all together, and we were Gay. Dykes and fairies, freaks and hairies, butches and drag queens throwing bricks at the police. *Thunk.* "We're Gay!"

But right away The Lesbians had a problem. They wanted to be separate. So we became Gay and Lesbian.

They had a point. They needed some space, after eight thousand years of getting shit from the PWP (People With Penises).

Pre-op transwomen set them straight. "We're not the oppressors. It was DWD. Dudes With Dicks."

Ignoring them, a couple weeks later, The Lesbians had

another problem. They said, "Women are more oppressed than men. So we're first." So we changed it to Lesbian and Gay.

But fags were like "Nuh-uh, Miss Thang. Ladeez first." So we changed it back to Gay and Lesbian. In the beginning, we only had two words. We didn't need to abbreviate. That was about to change.

B IS FOR BISEXUAL

One thing that hasn't changed is how well we get along. In San Diego, fags rule: GLBT. In San Francisco, hags rule: LGBTIQQ. San Francisco queers hang out at the LGBTIQQ Center. We didn't want to leave anyone out so we kept adding letters. Then we couldn't afford to change the sign every week, so now we just call it "The Center." Okay, what letter were we on?

You know how it is when you get pulled over for drunk driving? "Can we get you to recite the alphabet, sir? Uh, ma'am?"

And you're so drunk and it just seems so long, you can't remember unless you sing it, "ABCD...," while touching your nose and standing on one foot, and the cops are laughing so hard they let you go? Any time you have to remember a bunch of letters strung together for some inexplicable reason, sing them to the tune of "Twinkle, Twinkle, Little Star."

LGB... Oh yeah. B, for Bisexuals. Everyone hates The Bisexuals.

"They exercise heterosexual privilege half the time. A walking swinger bash: girl on one arm, boy on the other. Party in their pants, everyone's coming."

That's not even true. They usually switch off, one at a time. "Boys are stupid. Time for a chick. Chicks are high drama. I need stupid sex, no questions asked."

Some think bisexuals are more enlightened. But most people are just jealous of what they think must be a non-stop orgy. There's no need to be jealous. Think of all the people you could have boinked if you were cool enough: Marlon Brando, Drew Barrymore, Angela Davis. De Beauvoir, Dietrich. Garbo. But no.

We bring shit to throw at 'em at the Pride Parade. "Look, there's the bisexuals!" Throw a dead cat. "Fuckin' bisexuals."

In reality, poor bisexuals can't get a break. If you're bi, your dyke exes will talk to you at parties, smiling daggers. "Oh, you're marrying a man now? I heard the two of you just wrote a book called *Dyke Sex Secrets for Men*. How nice. In a world where there are only two female CEOS in the Fortune 500, no female president yet, and our president gets to be married to the butchest lady around, I'm so excited to share the only thing I have going for me that men don't: knowledge of the whereabouts of your G spot."

T IS FOR TRANNY: A BRIEF HISTORY

T stands for "tranny," which is short for "transgender," which includes butches, queens, and other gender outlaws, as well as transsexuals, which are transgender people who actually change their sex.

For years, transgender people called ourselves "trannies." As queers, we inherited a camp sense of humor from transwomen of yore. We took the sting out of *dyke, fag, queer, tranny,* and other epithets yelled by 'phobes who were kicking our asses.

The rule is: you can't reclaim something you are not, unless you're a dyke talking to your best friend who is a tranny, and you say, "Girl! You're a hot tranny biotch!" And she says, "Shut it, keep your dick in your pants, you big dagger tranny-chaser."

Dyke, fag, and *queer* are somewhat assimilated into popular queer jargon, but, because the trans community is the last in the long line of queers to win acceptance even from the LGBT community, if you say *tranny,* even if you are a tranny, you'll still get glared at by middle class, educated, transfeminist trannies on high alert. So label yourself at your own risk.

When I was young, I didn't know just anyone could be a tranny. I thought you had to be a rich professional tennis player. When I got older, I was busy transitioning on crank, so I missed the underground hormone railroad. I knew about Diesel Dykes. Drag Queens. Dinosaurs. We didn't have all the cool transcultural gadgets and terms that have evolved over the last few decades, for example, *genderqueer* (proud label of those who refuse labels), or the genderqueer pronouns, *ze* and *hir.* We sure couldn't pick up a shot of hormones at the clinic without first having to admit we were crazy, but sane enough to transition.

Author Leslie Feinberg was banging testosterone, but ze was stealth, getting street hormones from South of the Border. If I knew Vitamin T was a drug that could make me a man, or that anyone was shooting it, I'd have been tracking hir ass down: "Hook a brother up."

Instead, when guys really wanted to put me down, they

said, "You just want to be a man." And I vehemently defended myself: "No, I don't..." I was a feminist. I was clueless.

I didn't have today's Transgender Brotherhood to show me the ropes, validate my inner dude, show me stuff like how to tape down the twins, strap it on, go to the barbershop and ask for a crew cut with a straight face, or wear boxers.

Fortunately, I came of age after Leslie Feinberg did in the '50s, when cops used to bust into bars and enforce the Three Articles of Gender Appropriate Clothing Law. Three? If you had a man-gina, even if you were looking sharp in a suit, you had to be wearing some panties, a bra, and God-knows-what-else. Super complicated. A garter belt? How are you gonna wear a slip in a suit? Could you cheat and wear three pairs of panties?

In the '70s, I may have been working without any supervision, but I was not gonna wear any goddamn panties. But boxers—whoa!—I didn't know you could wear boxers. Nothing came between me and my 501s. And I didn't make it to the laundromat a lot, as I was busy getting laid. So I measured my sexual prowess by my crotch seam snail track.

At this point you're thinking, Snail tracks? Was this guy raised by wolves? No, I was raised by Castro clone fags who wore no underwear and sandpapered their denim crotches to create what looked like a rubspot from their massive members. I was also raised by queens, male-bodied people who dressed like women, but didn't medically transition. They just lived their lives as women, performing drag at Finocchio's by night, shopping at the mall by day, in wigs, falsies, and hubba-hubba heinies.

Lines were blurry. Everyone called each other *Girl*, *Girlene*, and *Mary*, but some of us received these terms of endearment more earnestly than others. Nowadays, don't call a transwoman a "drag queen." Handbags will be swung.

IN OUR FAMILY, APPARENTLY, HATE IS TOO A FAMILY VALUE

I grew up watching my pals, the queens who were transwomen (but didn't call themselves that yet), go by on their Gay Pride Parade floats with their queen wave: elbow elbow, wrist wrist wrist.

I'm for anything with feathers and tits, even if it's a water balloon. I'm a known drag racer, tranny chaser. They always see me coming. "Watch out, here comes the copafeeliac."

"Copafeelia" is a new category in the DSM (the American Psychiatric Association's *Diagnostic and Statistical Manual of Mental Disorders*), between "Anxiety" and "Gender Identity Disorder."

Shrinks are as good as cops at keeping us in line for our own good. Whatever you are, they've got some way to pathologize you, just in case they ever need to come after you and send you flying over the cuckoo's nest: straight dudes that are too masculine; straight chicks that are too feminine; straight men that crossdress or become women because they think it's hot. According to the DSM: crazy, crazy, crazy. Cray cray. Craylene. And you thought you were safe, all you footballers, cheerleaders, and Ed Wood.

So back to the Pride Parade, with my crazy self—flying my freak flag, extremely charmed by the beauty queens riding by on their floats. Next to me, The Lesbians are hating: "They got dicks. Oppressors! Throw a dead cat." And lesbians love cats so when they throw dead cats, you know they're pissed. "Having fun?! Womanhood is not fun! Let's go watch the boring speeches."

On the other side of me, The Gays are hating the queens, too. Straight-Acting Gay Guy yells, "Hey! You're making us look like flamers. We are trying to assimilate so the Christian Right will love us."

And the Log Cabin Republican takes the Straight-Acting Gay Guy out of his mouth long enough to say, "Yeah, we wear suits just like straight men! Now everyone's gonna know we take it up the butt!"

And the MSM on the DL—who isn't gay but merely a Man who has Sex with Men on the Down Low—stops drilling the Log Cabin Republican to say, "Yeah! Damn bitch! Wait. Is this the *Pride* Parade?" and pulls out. As he walks off, the Republican says, "I always know when I'm in love, 'cause when he pulls out, it goes *pop*."

THERE'S NO "I" IN *TEAM*, BUT THERE ARE THREE IN *GENITAL MUTILATION*

LGBT…. That's where the acronym used to end. But now we just keep going. Someone threw a vowel in there, trying to make the acronym pronounceable.

I is for Intersex. Intersex means you might have both male and female physical characteristics. One of the main issues intersex activists have is with doctors who make it so you can't ride a bike or have a decent orgasm. But doctors are trying to help. They are so helpful.

"Push, that's right, push! Breathe! You got it, congratulations! It's a..."

Doctor Genderright stops, looks at the genitalia of the child, confused. Excuses himself and steps out a moment, babe in arms. We hear singing. "Easier to dig a hole, honey honey, than it is to than build a pole, babe babe." He makes minor adjustments in a backroom with butcher knives and eggbeaters. Hands the kid back. "... girl!"

The Radical Cheerleaders jump in with a cheer about the right to use the human body you were dealt any way that makes sense and feels good doing it, whether it's painless bicycling or orgasmic shagging. We don't care about a white man in a white coat.

"Drop the eggbeater, Doc, and step away from the genitalia, nice and slow. We like long clits and short dicks, fancy chromo combos, so much clit she don't need no balls. Step back, Jack, the babies are staying intact.... don't fuck with my babeez..."

Only it rhymes and makes you wanna make a touchdown.

QUEER AS *GET THE* FUNK *OUT OF MY FACE*

LGBTI... Q. Does that stand for Queer? Nope. Questioning! You got questions? "Oh my God, does that circle jerk back in '85 mean I'm gay?"

Questioning? Sure! Everybody! Pile on! Do you surf celebrity porn and jerk off? LGBTIQJO! You get your own float.

"I identify as a question mark. My pronouns are *whatthe* and *fuck*." Sure, LGBTIQQJOWTF.

Okay, no really. Q does stand for Questioning. But... In case

LGBTIQ doesn't add up to Queer, we actually added *another* Q. We don't have enough letters in the alphabet to represent all of us, so now we're gonna double up. Because Q might mean Questioning to you, but it means Queer to me, so let's add an extra Q. For "Queer."

That's right, LGBTIQQ. More random letters than an '80s sports car. SEX 2000. 450QRZ Turbo Minivan. Gonna soccer mom all over town so fast, I'm gonna ace that Soccer Mom Indy 500 in my LGBTIQQJOWTF 5000... I'm going so fast I can't even see my own reflection in this community.

QQ. This is gonna come to no good end.

DOUBLE DUTCH

Time for the community to discuss. Bring out the pig and the pirate.

Pirate: "Wait, the B for Bisexual doesn't represent you?"

Pig: "Nope."

Pirate: "I heard you got your first BJ when you were 13 from your dog, Brownie."

Pig: "Yep."

Pirate: "How'd you do it?"

Pig: "I smeared some peanut butter on my dick."

Both: "Add a B! for *Bestiality!*"

Pig: "I heard you like to wear diapers and crawl around like a baby."

Pirate: "Yep."

Pig: "That's hot."

Pirate: "Ga-ga!"

Both: "Add an I! for *Infantilism!*"

Pig: "You only like to be on the receiving end of BJs?

Pirate: "And you're a pillow queen?"

Both: "Add an extra L for *Lazy!*"

Pig: "Let's freestyle!"

"BB! LL!"

"I'm special and unique!"

"I need my own letter!"

"I'm sensitive!"

"You shut up!"

"No, you shut up!"

Pig says, "Hey! In Chicago, they added an A. For Allies."

Pirate says, "In Manchester, England they add an A for Asexual."

Pig says, "We need a new acronym."

"Right?"

"How 'bout PWDVFB?"

"What's that stand for?"

"People Who Didn't Vote For a Bush!"

"Ummm... "

"It's more inclusive."

"It's outdated."

"It's retro."

"It's unpronounceable."

"So's yours."

"Yours is more so."

"No, it isn't."

"Yes, it is."

The small dog dressed as a baby snow seal pipes up, "I identify as a Furry."

The sheep chimes in, "I'm Transspecies."

I offer, "I identify as an Extraterrestrial."

Snow seal turns to me. "Phone home."

I say, "No, you phone home."

The sheep says to the seal, "Yeah, you phone home."

The seal says to the sheep, "No, you phone home."

They get into a stuffy moshpit and try to kill each other.

Hang up and drive.

APPROPRIATE THIS

Queers. We love each other. And we ask better questions. We would never be so gauche as to ask if you are a man or a woman. No, we ask, "Which pronoun do you prefer?"

"Why, thanks for asking. *Shim* and *herm*."

Then use it in a sentence. "Is shim going on a hot date with that babe? Shim better bring herm's rubber dick."

Then everytime we go somewhere with the person, we have to ask, "Which pronouns do you use in front of your parents - old high school buddies - colleagues?"

I got a little nudge from The Gender Police the other day, someone who was not actually intersex, but was just a supporter, watching out for them. The Gender Cop wanted to know if I knew that "herm" was a word intersex people are using to describe themselves.

I said, "Yeah, I'm buddies with the president of ISNA, the Intersex Society of North America, and she gave me permission to appropriate intersex culture. I'm a professional cultural rip-off artist, San Francisco's own Mandonna."

Madonna rips off a new culture every year. Catholicism isn't so exciting since they stopped burning queers, whores, and blasphemers at the stake. Madonna's like, "I'm gay! I'm Hindu! I'm Jewish!" Which is fine. Catholics and Jews are practically the same, with the guilt and all. Genderqueer and intersex are practically the same, with the ambiguity and all. "I'm both! I'm neither!" Sing it with me: "I'm every queerbait, it's all in me... "

Under the unpronounceable acronym, T is right next to I. We could share. Herms could use "shim." It would be like borrowing a cup of sugar as an excuse to be neighborly.

I'm going for the Hierarchy of Oppression tie-breaker at the Gay Olympics. Queers love processing. You know who hates to process? Guys. No wonder femmes leave butches for dudes. If guys ever do have a feeling, you never have to hear about it. Simple. A BJ in the morning, hand over the credit card, and Girl's going shoe shopping. Dreamy.

Men are so easy-going. Poor straight guys. You gotta feel for them. The only way they know they're in a serious relationship is when they no longer buy candy on Valentine's Day to get laid. They do it to avoid getting beat up.

Maybe I'll just appropriate straight white male culture. But true to appropriation rules, I'll only take the good parts: a T-shirt with a picture of Johnny Cash flipping you off.

WE STILL GOT QUESTIONS

"Do you identify as a man or a woman? A dyke or a transman?" Which all really means, "Whose side are you on?" The Lesbians keep up with rumors by using the LPT, the Lesbian Phone Tree. "Lynnee Breedpal has crossed over. Surgery next Friday. 1-800-LOP-M-OFF. Traitor to the weemoon."

Trans people and their supporters use the TPT, Tranny Phone Tree: "Lynnee Breedlove's calling herself 'he,' not even shooting T or losing the puppies. She's just a butch making a million bucks biting trans style."

Butch tapping the LPT for the CIA: "He did not say 'just a butch.' I will Aileen Wuornos his ass." When straddling the barbed wire fence between lesbians and trannies, it's good to be dickless.

The Feminists are trying to wrap their huge brains around

the Trans Thing. Their brains are huge from thirty years of processing. They can't get into their Volkswagen bugs. They say to me, "Wait, what's a transman? Is that the oppressor? Or is that the traitor?"

I admit, "I'm the traitor. But I used to be a woman–lovin' woman, now I'm a man-hatin' man." That's a lateral move.

CONFUSED, CONFUSED, DON'T WANNA BE CONFUSED

S ometimes when I am hanging out thinking about stuff, I like
to make a list of pros and cons:

TOP TEN REASONS TO NOT TRANSITION

10. Can have stuffed animals on the bed.

9. 24-hour breast access.

8. Femmes.

7. Save a bundle on hair removal and porn.

6. Save time and energy on wanking.

5. Access to clean public restrooms with doors on the stalls.

4. Stealth woodies.

3. Crying.

2. Can feel morally superior knowing fart jokes aren't funny.

1. Can get away with misogynist jokes and still blame men for
everything.

TOP TEN REASONS TO TRANSITION

10. Get to stay in the DSM, which is almost like being published.

9. Shirtless at the beach.

8. Queer girls.

7. Same job, better pay.

6. Get to freak out guys at the urinal: "Oh my God! My dick is gone!"

5. Fart jokes are funny.

4. Gay men and drag queens.

3. Go straight to sleep after sex.

2. No crying.

1. Upper body strength for lifting babes up and doing them like Vin Diesel.

QUEER THEORY

Lists don't clarify shit. You know who's always clarifying shit? Queer Theorists. They are really trying to clear things up. Like Judith Butler. She's clarifying like crazy. "Gender is two boxes. No... four; no... six. No, it's a line, with 'He' on one end and 'She' on the other. No, Ze and Hir, Shim and Herm, Argh and Ay, It and Them. No, that's not right. It's an infinite line. No, that's too linear. It's more complicated. It's a sphere."

I call her on the phone. "Hey, Judith. What are you talkin' about? Call me when you know."

I told her gender is best explained with Russian nesting dolls, those painted wooden dolls that have another one on the inside, and another one inside of that... The kind of toys that gave us hours of entertainment before we had *The Simpsons*.

My nesting dolls are Obi-Wan Kenobi—old man who likes

to give young people unsolicited advice; Courtney Love—washed-up rocker, oughta-be-ashamed-but-ain't; GI Joe—badass, looks good in fatigues, don't nobody mess with him, dickless; RuPaul—friendly queen; Frank N. Furter—mean queen. On the very inside, Peter Pan—an eternally small boy always played by a middle-aged woman.

IF DUCT TAPE DON'T FIX IT

So everyone wants to know what the hell is a tranny, then. It's someone who was born with one set of stuff but feels like they ought to have the other set and wants their outsides to match their insides. There are a lot of ways to go about this. You can be a transsexual and get surgery but that costs money, and most gender non-normative people aren't making the big bucks. If you're a transman, you can lop off the twins, but top surgery costs $8,000. That's a lot of lattés. Or blow jobs, I mean, massages. So on to options two through five.

For $30, there's a breathable compressor half-shirt. And you just tell the babe to call the twins "pecs," and negotiate a don't-touch-without-consent agreement. Everyone suspend your disbelief.

For $20, use the several-sizes-too-small jog bra, affectionately called The Bro.

Hate the gym? The neck-to-hips full-length compressor shirt gets rid of breasticles, gut, *and* love handles, for the lazy tranny.

Haven't had the operation yet: Pre-op.

Doesn't want surgery: No-op.

Just started transitioning? If you had a job, you're now fired. Unless you live in San Francisco, where if you work for the City, they'll pay for your medical transition. Everywhere else, between genders means between jobs. Better be nice to your girlfriend. If you blow it with her... for the homeless tranny, we got duct tape. That's not no-op, that's po'-op.

At five bucks a roll, you can wear duct tape for weeks in jail before it starts falling off. If you're banging T, your cupcakes—ahem, pecs—are gettting furry. Maybe you identify more as a gay pornstar than a bear. Just yank off the duct tape really fast, and, ta-da! Free waxing.

VITAMIN T

T is for Trans, but also for Testosterone. See, people, that's a two-fer. That's the direction we need to be going. I don't shoot Vitamin T. With my genetic makeup, I'd get a furry back and go bald. I'd be Tranny DeVito.

My pals are always telling me, "Hair on your back, none on your head—it's all part of being a guy. Hair poppin' out where you didn't know you had follicles. Babe magnet. Yaa, look! I'm a werewolf. " Well, then... I guess I'm just not committed.

I love the gay pornstar look. I secretly hope that all I have to do is bang some T to become a Brad Pitt lookalike with an 8-pack. But that's a full-time job of working out and hair removal. If T is on the menu, as a lazy tranny, I'd better be bear-identified.

My friends used to be dykes, now they're all fags. They'll do anything to avoid being straight. Now they're just as hard to convince to go out as when they were lesbians, "No, we can't go out dancing. We're shaving our initials in each other's butt cheeks." You got me. I'm not a real tranny. I'm a superficial metranssexual.

Not going bald is maybe the main coolest thing about being a chick. Between that and the G-spot info, I feel like Superman. I was bald once, when I came out. Not when I came out of the closet. I came out of the closet in the '70s. Big surprise. "Hey, Mom, I'm a dyke."

"Ach, nein! Reeaallllly?"

I wasn't bald when I came out of the closet because I wasn't a femme. When a femme comes out, she's looking like a straight girl. In order to get laid, she's got to shave her head, pack away her dresses, stomp around in engineer boots and a wallet chain while throwing rubber dicks at dykes. *Thunk.* "I'm gay!"

Me, I was bald when I came out... *of my mom's poontang.* And then I stayed that way for a year. Everyone thought I was a boy. If only I could have been able to appreciate those days. Youth is wasted on the young. Mom was not amused. Her quick fix: she attached pink bows to my bald head with Scotch tape.

THE BIZ

I was married once. I'd been nailing the old lady with the lights out for five years. She never knew I wasn't a cisgender dude. I Billy-Tiptoned her ass. One night she flicks on the light, points at the bro and the strap-on, and yells, "What the fuck? Explain yourself!"

"Fine... if you explain the kids."

In San Francisco, we use bumper stickers as political manipulation and self-expression: "I'M GAY AND I VOTE" or "I HAVE A DOG AND I VOTE." I want one that says "I AM A PUNKROCK FEMINIST QUEER TRANNY MOTHERFUCKER AND I RAISE CHILDREN."

I'm hangin' out with The Biz. She's five. If you're a commitmentphobe who likes kids, just wait until your ex has a tiny and help raise it. That's called "ex-tended family."

"Hey, I noticed you're not using that kid right now. Mind if I take it to the beach?" Feed it a bunch of sugar. Hand it back.

The Biz's mom was a stripper I dated in the early '90s. She popped out a couple gaybies fifteen years later. She made sure they were girls. Not 'cause she doesn't love men or anything. Strippers love men. That's why they strip! Can't get enough! Sure, dude. It's not for your money, no, she loves you. Really. Don't cry.

So the Biz's mom reads this book on how to make girl babies:

1) Test yer poon juice every day, till it gets pasty.

2) When it's the right consistency, invite your ex-boyfriend over, with his current girlfriend.

3) They go in the bedroom down the hall from you and your current girlfriend.

4) They fill a jar and she yells, "Got milk!"

5) Your current girlfriend runs down the hall and returns with the elixir.

6) You stand on your head.

7) She whips out the turkey baster, sloshes it in, and...

8) Boom-ba: girl gaybies.

The pregnant dyke moms are so psyched to tell you all the details. "Feel it kick! Look! You can see its little foot."

Yikes. *Alien.*

Then they invite you to watch them pop it out. "Come to The Birthing! It's gonna be a major rager. Party!"

I want to watch you give birth like I want to watch the

tattooed people hang from their back skin by hooks. Ouch. That's an entrance, not an exit.

So your ex pops one out. You're an instant parental unit. Pick from a list of titles depending on how much you want to be involved: Dad, Momma, Mommy (otherwise, when the kid yells "Mom!" they both come running every time—it's maddening), Auntie, Uncle, Godfather, Babydaddy. I looked at The Biz when she was born, "You're like me! Acne *and* wrinkles!"

She loved me, too. I knew this because she told me, and here's how. We named her The Biz because she was busy. We also wanted to see what would happen if you raised a kid with a determiner in front of its name. Mainly we named her The Biz because she was busy talking ISL. Not ASL, American Sign Language, but ISL, Infant Sign Language, or, since every baby's got its own system, Individual Sign Language. (See? Another two-fer.) I watched The Biz's mom decipher the kid's desires by shoving random items in her direction.

"Toy?" Synchronized hand waving out to either side.

"Bottle?" More waving.

"Breastaurant?" Waving stops. Milkbar, please.

A-ha. It means "I want." Maybe she's gonna grow up to be a femme.

THERE ARE NO GOOD BUTCHES

Don't get me wrong, for every high maintenance femme, there are three service-oriented butches trying to give her everything she wants.

Femmes are all, "Really? Is that so? I don't see any butches." (Shades her eyes, scouting the area.) "They're all becoming men. Okay, there's three—one of whom is drunk. The other two are gay, and they're doing each other."

Femmes, you just can't see the butches because you're standing on their heads.

"Ow, ma'am? Your stiletto. It's in my eye. Sorry." Butch whips out a hankie. "Let me wipe that blood off your shoe for you."

CURTAIN CLIMBERS

I don't want to pop one out myself, but I love anklebiters. Whompers. Small mischievous but irresistable beings. They've got a whole different angle. Constant source of inspiration. You just follow them around writing down everything they say. Boom-ba: you got songs. 'Cause you know what's better than inspiration? Copying.

WHOMPERLANDIA

"No Adults Unless Accompanied by a Child."
Bears,
They like to live somewhere else,
Separated from people.
Could a dog eat a bear?
Could a bear eat a dog?

Why?

I'm wide asleep.

Are you a little man?

No, I'm a little window.

Are you a surrealist?

Yesh,

One to hold the giraffe,

One to throw the radio in the bath.

Whomperlandia

Raise yer hand if yer cute

I'm cute.

Whomperlandia

Tigger suits and romper boots

What amazing kids we're raisin'

Small hands waving

Welcome homo

Exiled fruits.

The doggie was lello

And he ate a piece of paper,

Turned bright orange and ate

14 jelly beans.

One time a day

It likes to be listened to.

If the baby comes over

I will bite it.

But I did it anyway.

Now what?

You're mad but you still love me.

No mine, no mine

I want my Lynneeeeee

Who's the greatest pop band of the '70s?

ABBA!

This is all I ever need.

Whomperlandia

Raise yer hand if yer cute

I'm cute.

Whomperlandia

Tinies in Superman suits

Moshing in a circle

Kissing the Madonna CD case

She's my kid

She's cool, she's ace

But I'm never gonna sleep.

Sea lions look like cats

But they sound like dogs.

Bla bla black sheep,

Have you any wool?

Yessir yessir,

Three bags full.

One for the sock,

Trust me, I'm a doctor.

Don't trust me,

I'm a lawyer.

I'm always brilliant, I don't change.

I just stay brilliant forever.

THERAPY JAR

Parents are personal trainers. They only know one thing, and that's they don't know squat about training kids. And they were trained by four other amateurs who also didn't know squat.

It goes all the way back to Adam and Eve. Look at Cain and Abel. That's the worst parenting in the long, sad history of bad parenting. First ones out of the gate: one's a murderer and the other one's dead. 0 for 2.

And we haven't learned anything since. The only thing you do know as a parent is that you will find out how bad you messed up in thirty years, when your kid gets professional help and you get a detailed report, complete with guilt trip. Everything you do, you're saying to your kids: "Watch and learn." So start a therapy jar now.

Like when I was walking down the street the other day, and there was the cutest little three-year-old kid walking my way, trailing behind his mom. She turned around and said, "Keep up, will ya? Don't let the nasty man get you."

The little kid looked all traumatized. (Time for a dollar in the therapy jar.) I was flattered. She called me a man—I passed!

BAREBACK MOUNTAIN

Without knowing it, my straight dad taught me to be gay. Favorite musical: *Oklahoma*. Favorite entertainer after Michael Jackson messed up: Ricky Martin. Favorite western: Spaghetti.

Dad, hands on holsters: "Wanna see the fastest gun in the West?" Hands don't move: "Wanna see it again?"

Dad's nesting dolls: Squint Eastwood—badass cowboy; Charles Bronson—badass cowboy; Mae West—closet drag queen; Tiger Woods—golf genius; George Carlin—comedy genius; Flip Wilson—comedy genius that makes fun of drag queens; Ricky Martin—entertainer that babes want but can't have; Heath Ledger—badass cowboy that gays want but can't have.

My parents tortured me by taking me to the California

Oktoberfest as a child. My dad wore lederhosen, and me and my mom would wear matching outfits, which sucked, 'cause the only thing more humiliating than a boy in a dress is a boy in a dirndl. I wanted to wear my lederhosen which I had since age three. By age eight, they were wearing dangerously thin. I took them to the shoe repair guy regularly and had him patch the ass. By age eleven, my mom wouldn't let me wear them in public— as I'd grown out of them for ten years, my only official item of men's clothing had become hot pants. My dad's lederhosen fit him just right.

So this guy sits down him next to Dad at the long Oktoberfest table and says, "Hi, darlin'."

My dad thinks, *Oh, here's a guy like me who lisps and makes fun of gay guys.* So he lisps his "S's" and says, "Say, sweets."

The guy puts his hand on Dad's bare knee.

Dad jumps, "Hey! I'm married!"

Gay homosexual faggot says, "Oh? Happily?"

Dad, if you don't wanna be treated like that, why do you dress that way?

MISSED MANNERS

So the ex wants to know what title do I want in the ex-tended family: dad, uncle, godfather, or occasional pal. I said, "If I'm the dad when I take the kid to the beach, do I have to take you, too? I would need to call for back-up if I took two femmes to the beach. I'll just be the personal trainer."

One day I'm hanging with the Biz and suddenly I realize it's April 14th. I get up and say, "Oh, hey, I gotta go, Biz."

"Why?"

She's Questioning.

"I gotta do my taxes."

"What are taxes?"

"That's when the government takes your money and says they're gonna use it for schools but then they use it for war."

"What's war?"

"Well, that's when they send young people in planes and boats over to other countries to kill and maim other people."

"Main?"

"Maim. Blow off arms, legs"

"Why?"

You know, it used to be so easy. When we had feminism, we could blame men for all the lousy things: rape, global warming, war porn. Now we're all becoming men or marrying them. We used to be able to blame testosterone poisoning for everything that was wrong with the world.

Now people are shooting Vitamin T, whether they naturally produce it or not, and come to think of it, gay guys have always been loaded with it. It's suddenly apparent that it's not just hormones that makes one act like a mensch, but impulse control... something that does seem to come more naturally to women. When you want to bang someone over the head with a skillet, just rein it in.

We are born perfect, then the world starts right in teaching us to be unethical, narcissistic, sadistic little bastards. The less physical strength we have, the more we rely on charm and other forms of manipulation for survival. Then, at some point, we either learn manners... or we don't.

Even if we do learn etiquette, instinct can override socialization. An emergency can inspire ungentlemanly behavior just as easily as it can heroics. For example, studies show if you want to survive an airplane crash, be an adult male. That way, it's easier to shove everyone else out of the way. While some guys are doing miraculous water landings, others climb to safety over chicks, babies, and fags, who had better know how to stab a jerk in the ankle with a fork. Don't forget to toss flatware behind you, along with your high heels, before you jump onto the inflatable slide.

You gotta be a helluva personal trainer to raise a girl in this world. You can't protect them every second. So I say, "Biz, look, about 4,000 years before all us cool guys came along, a few assholes (put another dollar in the therapy jar), I mean, *jerks*, ran things, and they still do. So learn manners. Knowing which knife to use and how to use it will get you through this life. If a guy does pull a fast one, just grab your boxcutter and aim for whatever you can reach. Change this world, because it's the one we're living in. Be ready. Some men are gentlemen, and some are bullies. So don't be a man hater. Just be a man not-truster."

KNUCKLE SANDWICH

Everyone's telling you to worry about predators with guns,
So you scurry about limiting your fun
In the dark, when in fact the attack
Like a stab in the back,
Where you gotta watch your mouth
Is in your own house,
Love shack, Jackee.
Ain't no out-the-bush-jumpin' stranger
In the park
You gotta watch out for.
Just when you think it's cush, it's Mr. Danger,
Bite like his bark,
Kickin' it on your couch, yo.
You think a 12-year-old ho

Thought o' that on her own?

Why'd she run away from home sweet home?

In a pimp's arms it's better than it once was.

All her kiddie porn pals are dead in a dumpster.

If in the end she's alive

She'll a-been traumatized

Like 9/11 survivors.

Moms, what you gonna do when your boyfriend eyes her?

If he's a jerk

Call a high alert.

I got yer war on terrorists.

Fix yer man a sandwich.

Knuckle sandwich.

Is the orange juice queen back?

Bill Clinton,

Republican in a bad suit,

Just as whack.

Signing the Defense of Marriage Act.

DOMA?

No love for the homos.

Where's *my* princess bride?

You must be in a coma

If you think gay marriage

Is a carriage to hell

For society.

We need the Courage to Heal

From uncle dad's treachery,

Raising bambinis

For 21st century slavery machinery,
Penitentiaries cheaper than a factory,
Like what's fucked up by broken trust can be corrected
At correctional facilities.
All my homos in the big house
Came up in a hell house
Of rapes, beatings, shameful secrets
Generations on repeat.
How we gonna beat this?
It's so nice to have a man at least around the house
Feels right until his sanity goes down south
At midnight you gotta jam to your feet and roust the kids out,
Beat it from the beater and the heat,
Run away on an underground railway.
Wanted in 50 states, they say you snapped,
Kidnapped your own babies,
When bailing was all you could do to save them
From the raving madman sworn to protect them.
What's that about?
Dads diddling their children,
Killin' their women everyday,
Don't get half the space in the press
Of the one crazed babe
Who drowns the kids she don't know how to save,
While the front page raves how it can't explain
Why Maternal Instinct Turned to Rage.
'Cause babes are just plain unstable.
If he's so stable, why's a guy strangle

Chicks with his bare hands?

'Cause he can.

Judge is willing to let him serve two to six.

Chicks rebellin' with a gun or an ice pick

Will soon be chillin' on Death Row.

You gotta know kung fu to take a life.

You'll do less time than for a bullet or a knife,

Still pay more than a man who offs his wife.

'Cause what? Your life ain't worth as much?

Damn, make a stand

Like J Lo: had *Enough*?

Rough him up.

9, 10, he's out for the count.

Why you gotta be the one to leave your own house?

He ain't down.

If he's a jerk, call a high alert.

I got your war on terrorists.

Fix your man a sandwich.

Knuckle sandwich, knuckle sandwich.

NO VITAMIN T IN THE '60S

When I was a kid in the '60s, we didn't have T, but I always wanted my voice to be low instead of the chirpy little sound that came out whenever I opened my mouth. "Hey, Mom, when I grow up will my voice be manly like yours?"

"Sure, just drink and smoke a lot."

So I did, to bag babes by getting rid of annoying insecurities. If only I had known at the time, testosterone will cure all your ills. It's an antidepressant, anti-anxiety, ADD-fixing cure-all. You never see guys crying and depressed. They're all, "Yeah, baby, woo! Let's party!" It's chicks that are all, "Oh God, I broke a nail… where's that suicide hotline number?"

I could have used some vitamin T in high school, because as any transman will tell you, it can make you feel more energized, more assertive, less like crying, and it melts bodyfat right off your hips. We had something like that in the '80s. It was called speed.

I transitioned on tweak. It made badass man-muscles from my belly to my groin and nice boyish straight lines, but what kind of ruined the effect was covering my track marks with those full-length cocktail gloves.

Marching powder ruined me for hormones. Sharing your works compromises your liver so that it can no longer process the drugs which are actually designed for transition: hormones. I'm an addict. My mind is a dangerous neighborhood to hang out alone in, with a bag of syringes and a year's supply of anything strong enough to take the hair off my head and put it on my back.

FIRST HIT

The photo of a cute guy leaning over, with his jockstrap yanked down around his buttcheeks, lights up on the iPhone. "Who's that calling?"

"Jay. He's coming over to do it 'cause he can't do it himself."

Jay comes over. He's got that brand new transboy look, seven shots in five months, like a foal born standing up, a little fuzzy, soft... miniature of a mighty beast.

The Doc stays busy, keeps the patient waiting. If you want your shit bad enough, you'll wait. Doc is in no hurry. He has been on T for four years. The boy stands waiting, smiling, making small talk.

Doc, a metranssexual, hunches over a sewing machine swearing at zebra-print pieces of material that he is making into something to protect him from the wind on his scooter.

"Do you really think you're gonna go fast enough on that lawnmower to warrant that ridiculous item of clothing? I don't even know what that is."

"It's a—you know—neck piece thingy."

"Quit making him wait."

"Okay." He peels open the package containing the sterile syringe, puts it in the bottle, draws it up, taps the rig.

The boy pulls his pants down over one downy buttcheek. The needle goes in.

"Does it hurt?"

"No."

I study Jay's face for changes. Doc slowly pushes the plunger.

"When are you going to do it?"

"I don't know. I gotta think about it."

"You've been thinking about it forever."

"Yeah. When I do shit on impulse it's not always good. Already did this once before. Different stuff. Got me in trouble."

"Yeah, but this is different. You gotta be with friends."

The apartment is filthy. I empty the cat box like I do every time I come here. I put water in the bone-dry cat bowl. Put the cat in front of it. He laps the water up like a dog.

"Come on."

"You know that video on YouTube where I say feminists tell me I'm not a real feminist and I say, 'Suck my dick'?"

"I love that."

"Some guy said, 'Don't say "tranny," ' and 'It takes more

than a suit to be a man,' and my feelers were all hurt. Then I realized, he's just pissed 'cause I'm more man with tits and ass than he'll ever be with a beard and pecs."

"Yeah. They hate you."

"Yep. Okay, let's do it."

"Jay, go get some T for him."

"D'accord." He comes back an hour later.

I ready myself. I want to do it. I want control. I want an alcohol swab. There aren't any. I have to wash the area with soap.

Doc's gloating, gleeful, like all the other pushers in my life. But this dealer is different. This hit will not just make you feel okay finally. It's the first step on the road to yourself. You always expected to grow up to be Clark Gable. Now you're just *Misfits* Gable instead of *Gone With The Wind* Gable. (Still a stud in Marilyn's last flick.)

Spike's in, can't feel shit. That was easy. Doc pushes the plunger. "Does it hurt?"

"Nah." I could do this. I'm no stranger to needles. I got a high threshold for pain. But we'll allow pals into this circle, this first time. Maybe last. Maybe only an experiment.

"Finally some action." Doc's been waiting for this for three years. I get high-fives all around. Another initiate to the brotherhood.

I go outside. Just starting to rain. I ride home on my bike, looking into the faces of men. Do they look like brothers yet? Not yet. But human. Thunder and lightning. Rain soaking camo jams.

I run up the stairs, a little more energy, not much. I'm no teenage boy. This is no fountain of youth.

Rain pours down, and lightning and thunder crash, signs from *Frankenstein*. I do push-ups in front of the open window, and the blood and rain rush in my ears like a hit from a whipped cream can.

Timing hot flashes. I get out the yoga ball and do crunches, push-ups. Eyebrows and boy hips would be cool. Grow back that shit I yanked out in a last ditch effort to be a girl in '76. Get rid of the hips I grew on a 35-year chocolate chip cookie binge attempt to leave a body that wasn't mine. Over fifty percent of all transgender kids self-harm if they don't transition before 20. Oh, that's what that was.

I think I'll skip the mustache. And I'm definitely getting a Brazilian, from the neck to the bootay.

OH MY GOD, SHOES

When I was old enough to talk, my first sentence was, "My name is Johnny."

My mom said, "More pink bows." She got on the phone. "Charm school?"

Operator: "Yes. Can I help you, sir?"

"It's an emergency. All the Barbies have crew cuts."

"Hey, Mom, I need a drum set."

"No, you're going to ballet school. You valk like a drunken sailor."

Of course, ballet school kicked me out for dancing like drunken sailor.

The Biz identifies as an FPB: Fairy Princess Ballerina. First time I took her to class, I cried the whole hour. All the moms were looking sideways at me, *What's he crying about?*

To those moms I'd say, "Because! All her anti-Barbie, ballet school dropout, punkrock, feminist parental units who'd rather stab themselves in the eye with a fork than wear pink are standing up for her right to wear a tutu."

The main difference between me and The Biz is shoes. At three, I knew about shoes. You lose one, and the other one ain't worth shit. The Biz's first word: "Shoes." First sentence: "I need to go shoe shopping."

"You already have 20 pairs."

"I need 21."

We walk into the store. She's in heaven. Enthralled, she makes a beeline for the clear straps with rhinestone flower designs across the toes, lucite heels full of little red plastic fishes swimming around in blue water. She was born knowing this trick: you keep on the fab shoes you've just purchased—"I'll keep these on, thank you"—and hand your old tatters to the guy to put in the box.

She's mincing down Mission Street in her Minnie Mouse dress and dream heels. She gets home and whips off her dress, and she's prancing around, singing, "I got new shoes, I got new shoes."

Her mom says, "With those shoes, you have to wear clothes."

"Why?"

"Just put on a damn dress with those shoes."

The Biz puts the dress back on. We put another dollar in the therapy jar.

POST-FEMINIST

Now that the dykes who were strippers—or were banging them—in the mid-'90s San Francisco queer renaissance are all becoming (or marrying) men, women have become obsolete. If it weren't for straight girls and transwomen, chicks would be extinct. It's cool. Since feminists won the revolution, there's post-feminism.

Fomer dyke sex radicals—whether now men, gay, or just gay married—know a pair of stripper shoes when we see them. Which means we'll do a better job as personal trainers when it comes time to give our kids The Talk.

The average dad mumbles, "Well, you know, he's gonna try to get fresh, then we'll have to get you an abortion, so don't let him touch you."

But I'll be, "Hey, Biz. You know the pornos you dug out from under your mom's bed?"

Biz is bored.

"Yeah, it's cool, I'm not judging. You know that one where the chick's got milk dribbling down her chin?"

"Yep."

"And it looks delicious?"

"Uh-huh."

"That's acting."

Now that's gonna be some personal training she can use.

NO VITAMIN T IN THE '70S

Though I am reclaiming the boy I was at three, I remain a twisted rebel. We didn't have Vitamin T in the '70s, but we did have *Our Bodies, Ourselves*, the feminist Bible, telling you not to just tolerate, but love what the goddess gave you: tits, tang, and bingo arms. What're bingo arms? That's when your ungrateful kids throw your obsolete ass in the old folks' home. You are eating green Jell-O squares on a paper plate playing Bingo, and there's no use for money at the old folks' home—there's no shopping, there's no leaving—so you're playing Bingo for travel-size packets of Metamucil and Polydent, and when you win, you wave your arm around and yell, "Bingo!" and your once-fabulous triceps go *wabba wabba wabba*. That's Bingo arms. Without Vitamin T, Bingo arms are in your future.

So here I am, raised by queens on *Our Bodies, Ourselves*

to love my three holes and a heartbeat. Rejoice! Every month I bleed for a week and I'm not dead yet. Thank the great Gay Goddess! Tits up to here, tits down to there, cross-eyed, wall-eyed, I don't care. Gratitude and acceptance. God gave me this body so I could tell misogynist jokes without getting in trouble.

I'm used to working with what I got. Now along come hot young transguys, and I got teen idol envy. They got pecs. They're sprouting hairs on their faces. Biceps, ab-age, popping out everywhere. Lots of energy. You like teenage boys but you don't want to go to jail? Transguys.

Trannyboy math: Six daily crunches + one monthly T shot x 6 weeks = Six-pack. I do sixty crunches a day for six years, and I got a party ball. Pony keg.

Down the middle of my once-perfect abdomen, I have a six-inch scar though. Chicks dig scars. They want to know what happened. I tell them: I got in a knife fight with a surgeon. He won. It was only 'cause I was asleep. He heard about Lynnee "Don't Nobody" Breedlove. He did not fight fair. He said, "Hey, want some really fun drugs? Hold your arm out. Good, now start counting backwards."

I used to have a colon, now I got a semicolon. It's probably my fault.

"Scalpel..." The surgeon spots my tat of the guy with black holes for eyes and the huge knife dripping blood onto the caption, TRUST ME I'M A DOCTOR.

"Wait, never mind. Chainsaw." Should have covered that with some duct tape.

"Sledghammer." If duct tape don't fix it, it ain't broke.

"Eggbeater." Don't leave home without it.

"Boxcutter." And always wear clean boxers.

"Staple gun." Because you never know when you leave the house if you'll get lucky, or end up naked on a guerney.

BELLY TRIX

I still get chicks with belly tricks. Before I had surgery, I used to be able to squeeze my gut into a bagel shape. Now that I got this scar, it's more like a T. Hey, I don't have to shoot T... I got T right here. Chicks dig it.

If that doesn't convince babes, I say, "Hey, what's this?" Then I grab both sides of my gut and yank each handful of flab alternately up and down three times and then yank 'em apart, sideways. Three up and down, once sideways. I keep doing that until they have a glazed-over look. "Naked lady hurdler!"

That's a babe magnet. Chicks climbin' up my leg. I have to say, "Off. Stop. Get back."

If they don't like that, I push both sides of my gut together, then turn around and moon them. "Look, I'm a palindrome. Same coming and going. Dealin' crack, front and back. Poker in the front, liquor in the rear. Or is it the other way around?"

Guaranteed hottie stampede.

Your abs are cut? Six-pack? You got little squares on your stomach? I got squares. I draw 'em on with a permanent marker. Good for long-range flirting. Looking really real. In a dark bar. A long, dark bar.

FAT MAN ON THE BEACH

So I strap myself down. Wrap myself in duct tape. Fluff up the eyebrows. How's my hair? I got an XL gut and XXL hips. Everyone's gonna know I'm just a butch. Worry worry worry.

So the other day I'm walking down the beach and coming the other way is a hairy, old, fat man in nothing but a Speedo, sandals, and black socks. He's not taping anything down or on, or waxing his back, or Rogaining his bald spot, or sporting a combover. He hasn't been doing lipo or crunches. He's letting his pregnant-with-Budweiser-child belly hang over his little American flag thong, rendering invisible his blank-shooting package. He's smiling. He's proud. He wants everyone to see his roly-poly, furry, little self. Oh. My. God. That's *Our Bodies, Ourselves*. That guy's a feminist. So I break into song and I ask him to sing along:

BREASTICLES

I'm a boy.

I got boy boobs.

Breasticles like testicles but higher.

In the hierarchy of male identity

I feel dead.

They be sendin' me to the periphery

'Cause I eschew surgery

And vitamin T.

I got no money.

Already had my body modified,

Traumatized, needles and knives.

'Cause I'm no-ho

No hormones

No-lo

No lower surgery

No op

No operations

I spell M-A-N

Balls.

Balls to the wall,

That's all.

Gonna start a support group 'cause

I need hugs

Called the Big Titty He-Man Woman Hater's Club

For big lugs bugged by man boobs,

Jugs.

We'll exchange tips on over the counter strapper-downers.

Flatteners.

Wrappers so your flappers

Don't impede ya

Get between ya

When your tryin' a-pound her into the ground

Missionary style but your mounds are drownin' her.

'Cause I'm no-ho

No-lo

No op-at-all.

I spell M-A-N

Balls

Balls to the wall

That's all.

I apologized

For havin' tits

'Cause I'm scared o' knives

But you got pissed.

I'm more attached to 'em

Than I was at first, y'know.

Don't take it personal.

Me talkin' 'bout me

Don't amount to cursin' ya.

I'm my own personal art project.

Self-obsessed?

That's manly, yes

But a real man ain't so sensitive.

He's confident.

My choice don't make me less.

Your chest don't make you best.

We just want a squishy place for our —

Stuff.

So live and let live and don't trip.

She don't even make naked feel fake.

Skin all raw from yanked duct tape.

Her gaze makes pecs outta cupcakes.

Some guys get pushed outta shape

By pretty boys feelin' shitty 'bout titties

But cut or not cut ain't cut-rate.

Outside changed or unchanged

Inside self-same top shelf maing.

'Cause I'm no ho

No lo

No op

You're not

We spell M-A-N

Balls

Balls to the wall

That's all.

FAIRY PRINCESS BALLERINA REALNESS

The Biz may not be a real FPB. I may not be a real feminist, or a real man. That's right. I'm Peter Pan. I'm the Velveteen Fuckin' Rabbit.

People say our family is not a real family. That The Biz is being raised by a bunch of dykes, fags, sperm donors, trannies, and one Berliner faux queen fag hag grandma who identifies as Marlene Dietrich. "That ain't a real family. That's a freak parade."

I worry about The Biz growing up in this world. I pick her up at ballet class. "Hey, The Biz. What do you tell your pals I am? Your uncle? Your auntie? Your friend?"

"No. You're my Lynnee."

I'm a stuffed bunny that's been loved into realness.

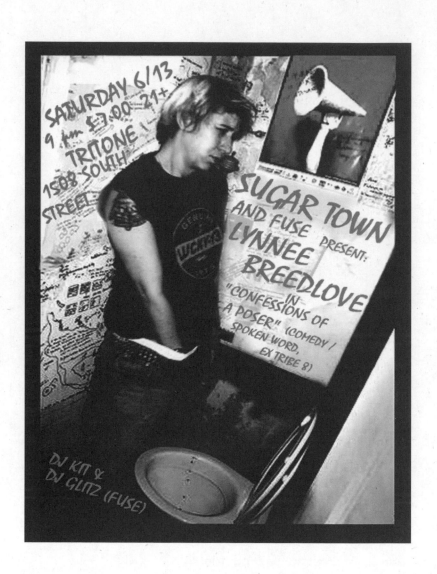

CONFESSIONS OF A POSER

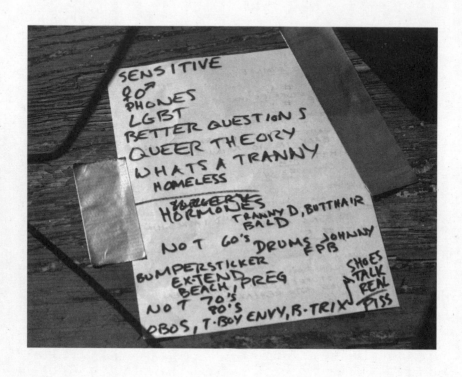

MYSTERY OF THE PURPLE DICK

Standing naked in front of the mirror with my cowboy hat over my junk. Hang it on my knob like a used bath towel. Put the hat on to reveal my outfit: a strapped-on purple choad, a dick with a circumference greater than its length.

"Honey? Does this make me look fat?" At least where it counts.

Names for boy junk are onomatopoeic. "Choad" sounds like what it is: a hockey puck. "Look out for that choad flying right at your head!" As opposed to "schlong," which is to say, hung like a horse. "Penis" seems small. You can say it through clenched teeth.

I don't have a penis. I have a cock, which sounds big. Have to open your mouth to say it. Especially if you're a New Yorker: "Ca-a-ack."

Examining myself in the mirror, I see the only reason I am not passing as a dude—what's giving it away—is the hips. I'll just slide some boxers on, nice and baggy, and boom-ba! No more hips.

No, what's totally giving it away is the harness. Slide the boxers up and poke the junk out the fly. Voila! Passing. Totally real. That's how I did that girl for five or ten years with the lights out. I think it was five. Just seemed like ten. We would still be together if only, when she turned the lights on, my dick hadn't been purple.

Why would you make a purple dick? Are the dick makers trying to help or humiliate? "Why" is not a spiritual question—it is what it is. The dick makers name all the dicks. The choad is called The Randy. Why would you wear a purple dick? A Eurobabe buys it for you.

She says, "In the US, purple is the color of lesbians, but in France, it's the color of trans."

Fine. "Here's your hot transman, all purple and proud."

Why do girls buy the purple dick?

" 'Cause it's pretty."

More like because they were out of black. That ought to tell the dick makers something. I like black because I'm Goth.

The real reason a girl buys The Randy is because it's shaped like a Dinty Moore stew can. The reason you make a rubber dick is to help you hit the spot. How am I gonna hit the spot—look, Ma, no hands—with a choad? It falls short. If I'm going to wear a purple dick, I need The Maverick, which is a schlong. Seven by two. Impressive. (Would be, if it weren't purple.) Curved up to hit the spot, not like the flesh and blood kind. You get them curved sideways, downwards, all kinds of directions that do not help anybody.

The Johnny is my favorite. Regular. Seven inches, curved up. All the help I need, since I am not all waving it in the air drunk at anything that moves, sticking it in light sockets and shit. The Johnny comes in human colors. (Not purple.) I like funeral parlor back room, dead-white-guy pallid. It's more dignified.

What are the dick makers thinking? "We need to sell more dicks. You know who's not buying dicks? Lesbians. They don't like dicks. But, boy, do they love purple."

What are they trying to do with the purple dick, help or humiliate? They are trying to help the Humiliators. You know, the girl that gets off on shaming you, then looks cute and innocent: "What?"

I bed this hot punkrock femme. Peel off her fishnets. Do the deed. Pass out. In the morning, I wake up to a funny feeling. I look down, and there is the babe, all focused, with her fishnets bunched up in her fingers, trying to get them on me. Not even, "Honey, I got you a surprise!" Just sneaking in there. Little face all concentrating, right next to my combat boots. Putting fishnets on my feet. Did she not notice my toenails were not painted with little daisies on them?

That's some fetish. It's called "feminizing." I didn't know it had a name other than "fucked up."

I'm all, "Have you heard of a thing called *consent*? You can't give your consent while you're asleep."

She's got all the bases covered. She's a pervert femme-inist.

She took care of that while I was asleep. I get up and look in the mirror. On my forehead is scrawled backwards in Sharpie, I CONSENT.

LIES I TELL MYSELF

I am a Cali boy, kind of woo-woo, into astrology and chakras. And yet kind of regular: I like the missionary position. I check Craigslist classifieds for someone seeking "extra romantical porn star to make out in the missionary position" in WSW, Women seeking Whatever.

I like the missionary position because once an Indian guru read my chakras, my palm, my aura, my everything. He said, "Men have got the lower three chakras going on: money, sex, power. Women have got the upper four: love and courage, truth, vision, godhood. So women are closer to enlightenment." And he ought to know, because he's from India. "But The Gays," he continues, meaning the unpronounceable acronym, "they have got all the chakras going on at the same time."

So when queers do it in the missionary position, we're all lit up like a Christmas tree.

But I worry, can I have tantric sex with a hunk of rubber? Do you have to have a flesh'n'blood body part inside another body part in order to complete the soul connection? Or is it like when lightning hits the puddle you're standing in but it doesn't kill you because you're wearing rubber soles? You can go manual, but there goes the chakra lineup. Your face is too far away for making out.

I worry. Am I real enough? Will I ever have as much fun as gender-normative heterosexuals in bed? Insecurity sets in. I do some self-soothing:

It's okay. His dick lasts only five minutes. My dick lasts millennia.

His dick averages five inches. Except gay guys. They self-report bigger dicks. (May be they're just bigger liars. Craigslist surfers beware.)

My dick is bigger, 'cause his brain is smaller... 'cause my chain is bigger, 'cause his chain is smaller... and I got two, because I have ADD and if I don't have two wallet chains, I lose my wallet.

My dick is germ free, adolescent. He's got a pigeon in his pants. Okay, mine is dirty when a babe wakes up frisky and wants it pronto, and I dig it out from under the bed, and it's all covered in dust bunnies. But nobody ever died from a dust bunny.

Mine tastes like banana-flavored condoms. His tastes like bleach.

But then, I am fascinated by penises and always researching

them on the internet. "I wonder what dicks are doing these days?" So I find out something his dick does that is fascinating.

His dick gives an oxytocin injection. That sounds like OxyContin for a reason. That's right, male ejaculate contains all kinds of hormonal goodies that trigger the release of dopamine and serotonin in the recipient's brain and get her hooked on his particular cock-tail, which she interprets as Love.

Never mind the Big Bad Wolf. This is a middle-school crack dealer sticking baggies through the fence. "First one's free."

A-ha! Now I can forgive the Hasbians: the only reason my exes go straight is because they're all junkies.

Could there be something to the old school radical feminist theory of marriage as sexual slavery, where babes blindly spend their lives polishing their chains? "Shiny! Pretty! Chains!" Drool...

That was before 21st century transwomen started marrying transmen and knocking them up. Nothing screws up power dynamics like a pregnant man.

My dick is feminist. It encourages a slow ride rocker babe's independence, when she gets up on it and creates her own happy chemicals in her brain. My dick keeps her free from a-dick-tion.

I'LL HAVE WHAT SHE'S HAVING

I did try men. I found a cute one that looked almost like a skinny girl: long hair, vegan. Don't let them convince you it's going to be sweet because they don't eat meat. I think it was me—running for the sink and spitting for a half-hour—who killed the moment.

Some people keep going back for more. All it took me was once. Someone hits me in the back of the head with a skillet and *KLANG!* ... won't be doing that again. If I were into pain, I would have said, "That's nice, can you do that once a day for the rest of my life?"

I guess I'm just a dyed-in-the-wool, vanilla, heterosexual vagitarian.

Mythbusters: what smashes the a-dick-tion theory to hell is gay guys who can do a different dude every night and be perfectly happy. Like having just one beer. Amazing.

But then there are the fags who would love to be hooked on cocktails—anyone's cocktail—and are jealous of lesbian merging. "Why can't I just settle down with Mr. Right? Why doesn't anyone ever bring me flowers?"

And then there are the would-be dyke womanizers, processing on the couch with the same babe for years, jealous of gay male sluttiness. "Why can't I bang a different babe every night, no strings? Why with the U-Haul every time? Why can't I have sex instead of talking about it?"

So maybe men are immune to a-dick-tion. Or maybe generalizations don't work. It would be so easy though.

WHEN DEL MET PHYLLIS

I'm walking through the Castro and I see the gay flag at half-mast. That flag is half a football field long, so when it's at half-mast, you know a VIQ has left us. I figure right away it has to be Del Martin, the Head Lesbian. Like everything she did, appropriate timing. This is the age of post-feminism. Butches are obsolete.

I came out back in '75, while hunting the sabertooth tiger, right after my graduating 9th grade class bequeathed a mirrored disco ball to Bancroft Junior High.

I didn't know what I would do if I actually caught a lesbian. I wasn't one of those people who came out of the gate knowing what to do in bed. I knew I wanted to kiss a girl but was at a loss for what to do beyond that. I searched feminist theory books like *Lesbian/Woman, The Natural Superiority of Women, Gyn/Ecology,* and *Chicks Rule, Dudes Drool,* for information on how to cook up a lesbian. Instructions were to be found in *The Joy of Lesbian Sex*, but I got triggered by bad drawings of hippies bumping topiaries. I slammed it shut and decided I was a kinetic learner.

There was a lot of Del Martin in all those herstory books though. She was busy. Phyllis Lyon met Del Martin and they moved in together in the Castro on Valentine's Day in 1953. Phyllis didn't even know she was a dyke until she met Del. Butches are always helping a sister *out*.

After a couple years of good times, they said, "Hey, we need some pals!" So they created the first lesbian organization, the Daughters of Bilitis. They called it the DOB, back when acronyms were still pronounceable.

Preceding riot grrl zines by forty years, in 1956 they wrote and printed up the DOB's first lesbian newsletter called *The Ladder*. In it, long before anyone conceived of gay marriage, they told women, "File your taxes jointly, as if you were a married couple."

Don't know why they called it *The Ladder*. Maybe because you could climb it right out of *The Well of Loneliness*.

Out at the bars, butch cab drivers surreptitiously slipped femme secretaries *The Ladder,* who took it to work, copied it and passed it on. Before laser printers or the internet, they hand-cranked out copies, called dittos. In the'60s, self-loathing eight-year-old queers like me sniffed up fumes from wet pages of pop quizzes in school like the cokeheads we were to become.

Adult lesbians loved that methanol alcohol smell of fresh *Ladders*, as they didn't yet have a problem with going to the bar, getting faced, and finding a life partner for five years. And the mimeograph ink was, conveniently, purple.

So in the '50s, instead of being stuck alone in the countryside getting depressed, women could go to San Francisco bars, get drunk, get laid, break up, and do it again, because thanks to *The Ladder*, there was an endless flow of babes coming from Peoria to the gay Mecca.

Del and Phyllis just wanted to create community at first, but that led them to crash the National Organization for Women, which from its inception in 1966 was comprised of all straight ladies. NOW's stance on lesbian inclusion: "Dykes? No thanks. We're trying to get women's rights here. You'll just fuck it up for us."

Del and Phyllis elbowed their way to the front. "Yeah, no. We're in." They convinced NOW to form the Task Force on Sexuality and Lesbianism in 1973, based on the notion that some dyke issues might also be some women's issues, as dykes actually were, maybe, women. The title of their 1973 book *Lesbian/Woman* sounds redundant now, but at that time, it was news.

Working to get shrinks to admit "queer" doesn't equal "crazy" and delete homos from the DSM, Del and Phyllis created a legal leg to stand on so dyke moms could keep their kids. Before that, if you decided to dump hubby for your lady friend, he got the kids, because you were an unfit mother with loose morals (read *dyke slut*, an epithet dyke sluts later reclaimed with pride).

Lyon and Martin had no idea how far their atmosphere of gender tolerance would reach. Trans-feminism would replace biological destiny. Feminists would become hot. Guys into anything beyond the missionary position would find room under the queer umbrella, learning the secrets of hasbians. As a result, feminists would smuggle the radical notion that women are people back to Peoria in a Trojan horse called straight marriage.

The more radical notion that we don't have to accept the gender assigned us at birth took longer to accept. Transwomen were regularly tossed out of women-only spaces, including the DOB, although not by our heroes, Del and Phyllis. That wasn't their style. They had already moved on to the next fabulous cause.

It took a couple of dykes to help straight chicks who got beat up by their husbands. In the '70s, straight people still figured, *You married the guy, you signed up for the ass kickings.* Comes with the dinner. You have to wear big sunglasses and say you fell down the stairs.

Del wrote a book called *Battered Wives*, coining the very term, *battered wife*. Before that, guys thought this was funny: "What do you tell a woman with two black eyes? Nothing, you already told her twice."

Feminism has come so far today, that joke is only funny when you change it to, "What do you tell a guy with two black eyes?"

Now that all the man-haters are becoming men, that isn't funny either. But this is: "How many trans-feminist men does it take to screw in a light bulb?"

"That's not funny."

GYNO-COLOGY

Until the '80s, dykes who needed a free twat-check had to go to Planned Parenthood and fill out a form that asked what kind of birth control they used. "Um, lesbianism?"

Coming out to a doctor armed with sharp instruments called side-biters and a cold metal speculum buried in you might seem worth a laugh. Dykes lived dangerously.

Lyon Martin Health Clinic, named after Del and Phyllis, became the first dyke gyno clinic. They guaranteed you'd get your stuff checked by a chick doc who was clued in to what might have been recently in or around your *area*.

They used plastic specula, and on the ice-cold metal stirrups were oven mitts. You could finally relax, feeling like any minute Aunt Mildred might bust out some chocolate chip cookies.

The only requirement at the Clinic now is that someone defined some part of you, at some time, as female. If you ever have been, are now, or will be a woman, you're in. They serve not just dykes, but anyone who might have trouble getting free and respectful healthcare, like tranny hoes, cisgendered sistah hoes, and pregnant men.

GOIN' TO THE CHAPEL

Then Del and Phyllis noticed that not only doctors and lawyers, but also clergy could use some guidance in how to treat people. So they started an alliance between queers and the church to stop hell on earth.

It's not like a lot of us care about going to the hot place. We'll be so busy shaking hands we won't have time to care.

But some of us actually do have a spiritual practice, and would like not to be excommunicated from the church of our choice. And in a country where separation of church and state is a myth that's winked at less and less, Del and Phyllis helped reduce the likelihood of the reinstatement of The Inquisition.

Finally, as little old ladies, in 1995 they were appointed to the National Conference on Aging and stood up at the White House against ageism. They'd lived together fifty years, fighting, as Del pointed out, the three C's: the Church, the Courts, and the Couch, when...

Wait, fifty? My parents could barely wait twenty. The day I turned eighteen, Dad handed Mom the cease-and-desist letter. "'Kay, bye!" Any monogamous cohabitation on my part kills the spark at three years. So the Christian Right can stop fantasizing about immoral perverts. After fifty years of sleeping together, the hottest date of the week is going to be side-by-side TV dinners in front of a *Simpsons* rerun.

Unless you're Del and Phyllis, in which case, somewhere, you probably have a photo op. And San Francisco's mayor, Gavin Newsom, had one in mind. Newsom is at the top of the food chain: young, handsome, straight, white, cisgender, and pals with the Gettys. Yet he's the guy who arranged the first gay marriages in California. He inspired people who never dreamed of wedding bells to line up around the block, a captive audience to Reverend Phelps' circling vans spouting "GOD HATES FAGS" and other Southern charms.

Gavin led Del and Phyllis to the front of the line, paparazzi cameras flashing. They doddered up the stairs of City Hall, took their vows, and cut the wedding cake to a standing ovation.

After a couple of years of California gay marriages, a whole new branch of divorce law opened up, and the term *gay divorcee* took on new meaning. And then the state annulled all the happy gay marriages. But then they gave it back. Then they took it away. *Psych!* And Del and Phyllis were back to whoring around like the adulterers and sodomites they were.

And the lawyers said, "But wait! It's like when black folks couldn't marry white folks!"

And black folks were like, "No, it isn't!"

Then the California Supreme Court decided it was unconstitutional to deprive queers of their right to be as bored in their monogamous relationships as straight people. So Del and Phyllis dragged their tired little old lady butts back to City Hall.

"I saaaaiiiid, I do, already," muttered Del, all snarky and cute.

"Yeah, yeah, I do too," said Phyllis.

They dutifully gave us what we all want, something to cry about. Too much vitamin T? Can't cry? Emotionally crippled? Check this out on YouTube: Del with her shock of white hair, no longer a young strapping dagger in a flannel shirt, now in a wheelchair, looking up at Phyllis, and Phyllis looking down at Del, all lovey-dovey. Quit crying. Man up.

Del died before The People took marriage away again. But the way in which they changed the world, no one can take that away from them.

MAN UP

My dad is an athlete, a pole-vaulter, a backpacker, a basketball player. Identifies as Burt Reynolds. If you Google images of Bob Breedlove, Burt Reynolds pops up, cradling a football in *The Longest Yard*.

Dad's always learning new skills. Learned to ski at age forty-five. Skis black diamond slopes at age seventy-five. Says if he keeps going at this rate, by the time he's ninety, he'll be skiing in the Olympics.

He's been a cowboy all his life. He wears cowboy hats with hatbands made from rattlesnakes that he killed and skinned himself. He taught me how to be a man which, in my country, means to kill things and eat them.

It's not like he isn't a sensitive guy. Not sensitive like "Ouch, quit it, you're offending my sensibilities," but sensitive like the kind of guy chicks love. A guy who finds a tire mark over the school lawn and across the cold body of our cat, brings him home and cries as he buries him in the backyard. But he cries like Clint Eastwood. Like he will kill a man if he ever finds the bastard who did this.

I was eight when I watched him shoot a pigeon off a roof and twist its head off with his bare hands, but only because it was suffering.

He has taken me backpacking with him since I was ten. On my first trip, I got to carry his very first 1946 wooden-frame backpack as an initiation rite, which I lugged, limping along behind him, while he bounded ahead lightly with his aluminum-frame pack. The canvas relic I carried had been ripped open and stitched up with dental floss, before he learned how to tie jerky up in a tree to keep it away from bears. Beasts, that is. Not hot, furry, gay guys with man-boobs.

You can only carry so much food, and you want to be in God's country as long as possible. So when a bear gets your mac and cheese, sometimes you have to kill something small and cute for protein. Or medium-size and ugly. Most guys Dad's age with their beer bellies and varicose veins can't keep up with him on the street, much less up a mountainside.

He says, "Do you know any young guys that can go back-packing with me?"

Yeah, I know one. I don't tell him Rocky is a transman, a 25-year-old, super-charming, hunk of an urban gym bunny with top surgery. Dad brings his 21-year-old nephew, Kermit, a straight, non-trans, city guy.

We go on a pack trip into the backcountry of Yosemite. My dad and Kermit were both born with stock parts. Me and Rocky are stealth. No one knows he's dickless, and no one knows I'm Peter Pan. It's a sausage party, half Not-Dogs.

REAL HOT

Rocky's been on T for eight years. He's super-fine and chicks dig him, as do fags and butches. He's just hot. He has had the discussion on the way out here, what pronoun does your dad use? I guess *she*.

Rocky, who always calls me "he," and respects my manhood and even defends it if necessary, is careful to always say "Lynn" around my dad and Kermit, no matter how awkward. "Lynn went to get some wood for the fire. Lynn said Lynn would be right back."

Rocky's chest scars are covered with fur. He's still not ready to go outside in public with his shirt off, but his torso is brown from San Francisco fake'n'bake—roof tanning, that is.

"What if people ask me about the scars?"

"Just say it's a failed pec implant."

I like to think if I went through all that to get rid of the puppies, I would be out every day swimming half-naked. If anyone asked, I'd say, "Hey, you didn't say I couldn't take my shirt off, you said I couldn't show the twins. I told you to quit looking at my tits. So… no tits. Screwed yourself out of a good thing. Ta ta, ta-tas."

But then I am a guy who only fantasizes about transitioning. In my dreams, I pass as a guy and when it's time to disclose, I have a plan. "Hey, did I tell you? I'm a yoga expert. Wanna see me give myself a BJ?" Then I'd take my dick out of my messenger bag and shove it in my mouth.

But Rocky's not taking his shirt off. He is bounding up the mountain like a deer, right behind the twenty-one-year-old, followed by the seventy-five-year-old. I'm limping along, bringing up the rear, glancing up at my team, three small dots at the top of the cliff. My knee hurts, I'm whining to myself, "Ow, this is hard, I gotta shoot some T. Hhmmm, I could just go to the gym. Nah."

Finally I catch up to everyone and we get to the slides, a long steep slope of slippery, white granite polished rock, with white water flowing over it.

"Hey, you guys! This is gonna be so much fun. Me and Dad have been doin' this for forty years, huh, Dad? Remember before you figured out that you had to wrap a foam pad around your ass before you went sliding down at fifty miles an hour, and you hit a ledge and almost got paralyzed? And your pals had to carry all your equipment for you so you wouldn't hurt your back? But you carried an empty pack to save face?"

As my mom always says about dieting: after fifty, you can't save your ass and your face at the same time.

"Yep." My dad strips down to his white furry chest. "I also remember when I used to take off my shirt, girls used to go *ooh!* Now they go *ew!*"

Then he wraps his foam pad around his ass and walks way up the mountain, tiptoes out on the slippery algae-covered rock to the middle of the slide, gingerly sits down on his blue foam strip, and wraps it around him. "Wooo-hoo!" He slides, 50 mph, to the pool at the bottom. Splash!

I follow him. "Yee-hah!" Climb out of the water like Pamela Anderson. "Come on, you guys!"

Kermit and Rocky look at each other, and then back at the fifty yards of slimy rock and pointy ledges. "Meh, not so much."

It's a hundred degrees, so Rocky tiptoes into the middle of the river to a rock and takes off his shirt. He lies out in the hot mountain sun for ten minutes. Then he puts his shirt back on and rock hops back over to me. "Do you think anyone could see my scars?"

"No, dude, no. Nobody saw. You look so cool."

Even in a strapper-downer and T-shirt, I am finally beating the man-o-pausal hot flashes, soaked in melted snow. In the mountains, you don't have to put your bro in the freezer. You can enjoy cold water and hot sun and mountain air on your bare ass, if you wanted, without any cops coming around, so I take off my shirt. I'm a man with tits. Not a real man, not a real woman, but under the big sky—equal to bears and fish and water and rocks—I'm real comfortable.

GONE FISHIN'

Kermit's a fisherman, so he gets some worms and pulls out five fish, *bang bang bang*. So I say to Rocky, "Hey, Rocky, you're trying to fit in more as a dude, right?"

"Yeah?"

"You want to quit all those old squishy behaviors like loving the bunny rabbits too much. How's that going for you?"

"It's hard."

"I know, pal. So, check it, I got a trick for you. All you got to do is learn to fish."

He's game.

"First, you gotta get a worm. See, now that we stirred up the pool, you just go snatch 'em up out of the bottom."

I go out in the water and catch six worms. I have to catch more than Kermit, because I am insecure and have to prove something. To whom, I don't know.

"See, on these guys, the head is too crunchy to poke the hook through, so you have to turn the worm upside down and impale it through its asshole."

Since my dad taught me this forty years ago, I—like Rocky—have become a Buddhist. I'm fucking trying. Starting out slow. Just not eating the cute food. No lambs, ducks, or plates of deep fried baby chickens.

But we gotta have some protein. So I get up close to the worm as I'm impaling it and sing, "Go to sleep, go to sleep..." I look at Rocky. "Wanna try?"

Rocky's traumatized. "No, thanks."

Dad overhears us and says what he's told me my whole life. "Give a man a fish, he eats for a day. Teach a man to fish, he eats for a lifetime."

"Yeah, Dad, we know."

Then I sling the line into the pool and yank it along until I get a bite, give it a wrist flick to secure the hook in the fish's mouth, then reel it in, fling it up on the rocks so it can't flip around and get back in the water. I pull the hook out of its mouth. It's gory.

"Okay, so now we're going to clean it. We don't wanna hurt the fish. So rather than sing it to sleep, we just smack its head on a rock." Whack. "Good night, little fishy."

I slice its head almost all the way off so its dangling, hold it on its back and slide the knife into its booty, slit the belly, grab the head, and pull the guts out with it. Toss the whole mess to the meat bees.

"Meat bees?"

"You know, yellow jackets. They got teeth. Chew right through a plastic baggie, eat all your worms and beef jerky. Chew your arm right off. Gotta keep 'em distracted with fish guts."

YOU KNEW I WAS A SNAKE WHEN YOU TOOK ME HOME

We're rock-hopping back to camp. "Look out, there's a rattlesnake."

Now I have always loved snakes, I am a Wiccan woman-loving woman pagan dyke snake-handler from way back. But rattlers are rather bitey. Not cute. They will mess up your whole pack trip. And they taste like chicken.

"This baby can strike from three feet away, and six inches up your leg. Somebody get me a stick, about four foot long." Kermit tosses one from a safe distance away, across the river.

I use it to pin the rattler's head to the ground. I saw it off with my knife. I poke the stick in its mouth, dig a hole with my heel, drop the head in the hole, and cover it up. "Gotta be careful, don't wanna step on that with your bare feet, still got venom in it."

Rocky and Kermit give the What Just Happened face. I put the snake around my neck to carry it, hands free, writhing around on my bare chest, all bloody and headless.

Dad says, "Skin that bad boy, make a hatband." To Kermit and Rocky, "You two look kinda pale. Good thing we're having meat *and* fish tonight."

When we get into camp, there's a bear. I'm all, "Oh, shit. Bear trying to get our food, move out of the way." Don't throw rocks. Bears are cute. Throw a pinecone. "Get outta here, bear."

The bear runs away, *Oh, no! Lynnee "Don't Nobody" Breedlove!*

Kermit and Rocky, relieved, rustle up some vittles. "Whew. Girl? It's so nice to have a man around the house."

Dad and I go over to a tree to take a leak together. I always wanted to do that with my dad, but I couldn't. Had to wave my ass in the air like I just didn't care about bears, snakes, and meat bees. Now that I am a tool, I have a tool originally designed for camping chicks to save their ass and face at the same time.

Dad knows about the *pisse debout*, and he's following the no-looking rule. Times like this I do wish I had that pack'n'piss'n'pass, so I could write my name in the sand. I can do it with the *pisse debout*, but I have to write in block letters.

"Dad, you know we all came up here to have a good time, a buncha dudes. But then we're old, or girls, or Buddhists. I think we might be leaving feeling a little less manly than the other guy. You know."

Dad says, "You picked up everything I taught you. You're not a whiner or a quitter."

"Thanks, Dad. Neither are you. Remember when I was forty, and you gave me your high school ring? That meant a lot to me. Better late than never."

Or as the queens told me when I came out at sixteen, "Better blatant than latent."

When I was little, I'd look at that ring in its little dish where Dad would leave it with his watch and his wallet, and feel like he was always near to protect me, but now, on my hand, it reminds me he's taught me to protect myself. I'm grown.

I hike back to the campsite, thinking. It was dykes like Del who taught me how to charm the ladies and make a boy with whatever's lying around the house. Duct tape and some Vaseline. And it was femmes like Phyllis who taught me how to tie a tie, hit the spot (no hands), and wear boxers.

They taught me that we can either hang together or be hanged separately. They put me on my logical gender evolutionary path: girl, boy, dyke, feminist, butch, man, badass.

A legacy isn't something you plan. You just do your best to show up in the moment for your generation and the next one, even if the kids totally don't get what you mean. They will take what you teach them and make it theirs, and you, the parental unit, better figure out something to like about it, because after they rail against everything you stand for, they need your approval.

Del and Phyllis taught me the heart is like a sphincter. If it's all clenched up, stuff hurts going in and out. Once your heart is open, you can't resist the cuteness of what you have wrought, even if you thought it was going to be women loving women, and instead it resembles tiny werewolves.

Those who came before us spent their lives making a world we all can live in. Without them we would not have mirrored disco balls. And we'll thank them by doing the same for Generation Whatever. Maybe we'll leave them with the perfect pissing, passing, and all kinds of other functional packie.

"Hey, Dad. Would you rather have a son or a daughter? It's not too late, you know."

He thinks a minute. "No. You're my kid. Here, need a cowboy hat? I got plenty." He salts the snakeskin for me and puts it out on a river rock to dry. "Your hatband will be ready in the morning."

In a world where no one ever feels man enough, I'm as real as any man. I stare into the campfire. Del brought Phyllis out, but Phyllis taught Del everything she ever knew about love. I bet she's missing her butch right now, even though Del's in everything we do.

I take a moment to thank a generation for a world where we can be whatever we are becoming.

GLOSSARY. If it's not in here, look it up.

Area - female genitalia

Billy Tipton - trans jazzman of the '40s and '50s with several wivees who claimed no knowledge of his trans-ness

Brazilian wax - from front to back, your area to your booty

Breasticles - breasts on a female-bodied, male-identified person

Bro - jog bra for flattening breasticles

Butch - N., Masculine lesbian. Adj., masculine, as in *butch queen*

Cyberskin - Porous synthetic material that mimics the skin of the cisgender male member

Cis - (prefix) As in *cisgender*, relating to gender assigned at birth based on physical attributes

Femme - Feminine lesbian

Fesbian Leminist - Proof of the existence of humor among '70s lesbian feminists

Maing - N., Nuyorican for "man"

Queer - Anything but straight, missionary position, 2.3 kids, and a white picket fence

Radical Cheerleaders - punk femmes who jump around yelling politically-edifying rhymes

VIQ - Very Important Queer

Well of Loneliness - 1928 tragic novel by Radclyffe Hall, banned in the UK for obscenity, about a female-bodied male (then called "invert") named Stephan who loses at love

Websites.

Freelax -www.consomacteurs.com/le-pissedebout-freelax-p-612.html

Mango Packy - www.mangoproducts.net/FTMPacking.htm

Pack n pee - www.mangoproducts.net/PackAndPee.htm

Underworks - www.underworks.com/products.html#996

Toys in Babeland - www.babeland.com

Thank You

Mom and Dad, for not letting me get a word in edgewise. I'm making up for lost time. And for loving me even if you don't know what the hell is going on. Bayla Travis for directing me. Sorry, I thought we were gonna get rich off this. Kriss De Jong and Eliot Daughtry, for making merch and doing all the genius things you do. Sam Berliner for editing the impossible video. Jim Fourniadis and Erin Ohanneson at the Dark Room, for putting me on stage and laughing every night at the same shit. Ren Volpe for encouraging me to do a solo show. Boo Price for editing, promoting, believing, and facilitating my transition from punk rocker to comic. Wendy Delorme for chasing me around Europe and promoting my ass to French skeptics for years. Thanks to the trans-laters: Sandra Ortman, German; Roberta Cortese, Italian; Wendy Delorme, French. Micah Rivera and Amy Cancelmo for deciphering the net and keeping me up to my ears in pit bull love. Alvin Orloff for editing with gentle grace and a queer ear. Apaulo Hart for cover art. Jennifer Joseph for patience and dedication. And all the girls and boys and everything in between that have inspired, supported, and booked me, and laughed at my jokes.

You make life worth living.